S0-ADV-484

WHAT OTHERS ARE SAYING

"With decades of Scouting experience and life lessons rolled up into one powerful book, Todd has brought to life the ongoing impact of the BSA."

~ *Pat Williams*
  Senior Vice President, Orlando Magic and Author of Extreme Dreams Depend on Teams

"I have said many times that I don't know a better list of worthy virtues than are listed in the Scout Law. We could argue over which one is most important, but wouldn't we be proud of our son if he exhibited even one of them? Scouting inspires boys to follow all twelve of these worthy goals which makes it unique among youth activities in these modern times."

~ *Del. Rob Bell*
  Virginia House of Delegates, 58th District

"Unfortunately, there was no Scouting activity in the Village of Big Island, Virginia, where I grew up. However, during my almost forty-seven years in the Virginia General Assembly, I have been privileged and honored to speak at several Eagle Scout Courts of Honor, and I have observed very closely the lives and careers of these young men. I am convinced beyond a doubt that the Boy Scout Oath has been a major and significant contributor to their successes. I have attempted in my professional career as an attorney, as well as the forty-seven years in the General Assembly, to conduct my life along the principles set forth in the Boy Scout Oath, and to the extent that I might have enjoyed some successes, the tenants of the Boy Scout Oath are largely responsible.

In my opinion, there is no finer youth organization in America than Boy Scouts."

~ *Del. Lacey E. Putney*
Virginia House of Delegates, 19th District

A Scout Is...
VALUES FOR A LIFETIME

Todd Shaw

SONFIRE MEDIA
A PUBLISHING COMPANY
SONFIRE MEDIA, LLC 2009

A Scout Is... Values for a Lifetime
©2009 Sonfire Media, LLC
Printed and bound in the United States of America

All rights reserved. Written permission must be secured from the publisher and author to use or reproduce any part of this book except for brief quotations in critical reviews or articles. For information contact:

Sonfire Media, LLC
411 N. Main Street
Galax, VA 24333

The Boy Scouts of America, all BSA images, the Scout Law, and the Scout Oath are Copyrighted Material. Used by permission of Boy Scouts of America. All rights reserved.

Unless otherwise noted, all scripture references are from:
Holy Bible, The New Living Translation. Copyright© 1996 by Tyndale Charitable Trust. Used by permission of Tyndale House Publishers. All rights reserved.

Other scripture taken from: Easy-to-Read Version© 2001 by World Bible Translation Center, Inc. and used by permission.

NEW AMERICAN STANDARD BIBLE®, Copyright© 1960, 1962, 1963, 1968, 1971, 1972, 1973, 1975, 1977, 1995 by The Lockman Foundation. Used by permission. American Standard Version. Public Domain.

This book contains information gathered from many sources. The printer, publisher, and author disclaim any personal liability, either directly or indirectly, for advice or information presented within. Although the author, publisher, and printer have used care and diligence in the presentation, and made every effort to ensure the accuracy and completeness of the information contained in this book, we assume no responsibility for errors, inaccuracies, omissions, or any inconsistency herein.

First Printing 2009
ISBN No. 978–0–9825773-0-1
Library of Congress Cataloging–in–Publication Data

DEDICATION

The Names

Robert Baden-Powell, Gerald R. Ford, and Neil Armstrong are all famous Scouts who made their mark on the world, inspired many young men, and contributed to the heritage of Scouting.

And then there are the local Scoutmasters and the countless other volunteers it takes to make Scouting possible at the local level. Their names may not be commonplace, but they too have a Scouting heritage; they too are leaving their mark on the world; they are the men and women of the Boy Scouts of America.

These tireless servants give of their time, and often contribute their own funds, to make the local Scout troop function as a unit that instills truth and knowledge: a unit where young men will learn to be strong leaders.

Why do they serve? Many serve because of the values of Scouting. Maybe they were not Scouts themselves, but were touched by the service of a Scout, so they serve to ensure that more boys are trained. Others serve because they were Boy Scouts, and they want to pass the legacy on to the youth of today. For one hundred years now, the Boy Scouts of America has influenced the lives of young men and their communities. In this book, you will hear stories collected from numerous adult Scouts — and stories of my own — about the life-long impact of Scouting. I hope they will inspire you.

* * *

I dedicate this book to the men and women of Scouting. Their influence in our communities, our country, and the world produces leaders with high morals and character.

In special dedication to:

Dot Godfrey, my Cub Scout Leader
M.B. Shaw, my dad and Scoutmaster of Troop 424
Troop 284, Galax, Virginia, my son's troop, where I serve as Assistant Scoutmaster

In memory of:
Vera Shaw, my mom and the spoon-swinging disciplinarian of Troop 424 and Virley Seay, West Columbia, South Carolina, past Scoutmaster of Troop 424

* * *

In honor of all the unsung heroes of Scouting, the author is donating a portion of his royalties on sales of this book to the Boy Scouts of America, and the Blue Ridge Mountains Council.

ACKNOWLEDGMENTS

Lisa, my lovely wife, you listen to my dreams, help me with my writing, and sew on my Scout patches. You are a great Scout mom and wife. I will love you forever!

Jason and Krista, my kids, you guys are the best and brighten each day of my life.

Doni Keene of Keene Ideas, my dear friend, you encouraged me in the early stages of this book and created the original cover concept. Thanks for your support and creative ideas!

Donna Triplett and Patty Moxley, members of the Joy Writers group, thanks for volunteering your time to read the manuscript and offer invaluable insights during the editing process.

Dan Johnson and Marla Baker of the Blue Ridge Mountains Council, thank you for your support and encouragement on this project.

To Eddie Albert, Brad Bradley, Paul Bragg II, Donald Capps, Jim Dalton, Bill Dial, Elizabeth Durham, Don "Big Daddy" Garlits, Bill Griffin, Dan Hayes, George Hicks, George Jones, Roderick Kohl, Bob Kornegay, Trace Lumpkin, Richard Marano Sr., John Matthews, Bill McCutcheon, Don Miers, Jim Moore, Jerry Schleining Jr., David Smoot, and Roe Young. Your stories have inspired me and I greatly appreciate your time. You truly understand that, "There is no limit to what can be accomplished if it doesn't matter who gets the credit." (Ralph Waldo Emerson)

Finally, to the team at Sonfire Media, Vie Herlocker, thank you for your countless hours of editing. I greatly appreciate your encouragement

ACKNOWLEDGMENTS

and support as you have taken on the task of making me a better writer. *Good luck with that!*

Larry Van Hoose, you are one creative man, for the final design, to the photos, from cover to cover, your ingenuity encapsulated my dreams for this book.

Sam Bartlett, you are a great friend and a man who truly knows how to liberate the greatness in others.

THE SCOUT LAW

A Scout is:

Trustworthy,

Loyal,

Helpful,

Friendly,

Courteous,

Kind,

Obedient,

Cheerful,

Thrifty,

Brave,

Clean,

and Reverent.

THE SCOUT MOTTO

Be Prepared!

THE SCOUT SLOGAN

Do a Good Turn Daily!

THE SCOUT OATH

On my honor, I will do my best
To do my duty to God and my country
and to obey the Scout Law;

To help other people at all times;
To keep myself physically strong,
mentally awake, and morally straight.

CONTENTS

FOREWORD
A Word From Zig

Some gangs are good. I realize that when you say the word "gang," most people react with fear, disgust, apprehension and other negative feelings. There is, however, a more positive view of the word "gang." One of the reasons young people get involved in gangs is because, across the board, they are accepted without judgment or criticism. There's a degree of loyalty in those gangs that appeals to young people. In addition, gangs have leaders and the members actually learn some leadership principles from those leaders. The gang member knows that he or she is accepted and there's a degree of security which goes with having some friends you can be with and with having your acceptance assured.

In addition to all of those things, some gangs have notable records of achievement. I'm thinking of one gang, for example, which produced eleven of the twelve astronauts who walked on the moon. It also produced a disproportionate share of Rhodes Scholars, college and military academy graduates, and business, professional and community leaders. This gang, with over four million members, also helps many youngsters find their niche in life through its "Career Discovery Program." Future doctors, lawyers, teachers, technicians and communications specialists, etc., result.

By now you probably suspect that I am talking about the Boy Scouts of America and you're absolutely right. A highlight of my life occurred when I was elected to the Advisory Board of the Boy Scouts of America, so I am now a member of that gang.

Question: Why are Boy Scouts so successful in life? Part of the reason has to do with the Scout Oath, the Scout Law, and the Scout Motto. I encourage you, especially if you are a single parent or if you are living in the "inner city," to get involved in the Scouting movement. For more information call the local chapter of the Boy Scouts of America. Take that action and —

I'll SEE YOU AT THE TOP!

Zig Ziglar

Example is not the main thing in influencing others;
it's the only thing.
~ *Albert Schweitzer*

Every father should remember that one day
his son will follow his example
instead of his advice.
~ *unknown*

Rules make the learners' path long;
examples make it short and successful.
~ *Seneca*

What can't be done by advice
can often be done by example.
~ *unknown*

CHAPTER 1

THE BEST CLASSROOM FOR LIFE

When I was a young man, I spent as much time as I could on my grandfather's farm in Aynor, South Carolina. I cherished my time with Granddaddy King because he made work an adventure; it was an outdoor classroom for life, just like Scouting.

One day on the farm, a sow got out and took her litter of eight piglets deep into the woods, and my cousin and I had the daunting task of bringing them back to the pen.

Being the great teacher that he was, my grandfather explained how we were going to accomplish this grand task — all we had to do was stand in the woods and catch a piglet. I didn't understand how that would work, but off we went to track down this three-hundred pound porker and her oinking litter of eight.

The trail was easy to follow because a hog that large leaves a wide and clear trail in the thick brush of the South Carolina woodlands. As we made our way through the thicket, I repeatedly asked how we were going to get the sow back to the pen.

My grandfather responded each time with, "Todd, when the time comes, you'll know what to do." He followed each proclamation with a deep chuckle.

I could understand catching those piglets, because I had done that many times in my young life, but the large hogs pushed my skinny frame around. Hogs go where they want to go, so once again, I asked, "How are we going to get the sow back to the pen?"

"Todd, you'll know what to do when the time comes." This time he sounded a little perturbed by my persistence.

We finally came to a clearing in the woods. My keen-eared grandfather held his hand out, a sign for us to stop. He made eye contact with us, and then pointed to the sow and her litter hiding in the brush a few yards away. Crouching down on one knee, he motioned for us to join him on the ground.

"Boys, I want you to be still. The little pigs are curious — they will come up to you. When you have half of the litter around you, reach out and catch one or two. Then I want you to take them back to the pen."

"But Granddaddy what about—?"

He didn't even let me finish my sentence this time. "Todd, you'll know what to do when the time comes." That was all he said, and his stern look told me not to question him again.

It was time for action. Our young hearts were pounding with great anticipation as my cousin and I took our positions in a small clearing. Within a few minutes, those curious little piglets came right up to us — the plan was working. I gave my cousin a wink of the eye, and in a flash we each had a squalling piglet by the back legs. Proud of our accomplishment, I looked to my grandfather for approval, but he was nowhere in sight. I called out, "Granddaddy!" and he peeked from behind a large pine tree with a suspicious grin on his face.

"We got two piglets, but how do we get the sow—"

This time Granddaddy wasn't the one who interrupted my question; this time it was a three hundred-pound sow charging us with her teeth bared and the hairs on her back standing up straight. She was a hog on a mission and we were in her sights. Panicking, I turned to my grandfather for more instructions.

He shouted, "Run boys, run! And whatever you do, don't let go of those pigs."

Sprinting and laughing, we didn't waste any time making our way back to the hog pen. You might say that we had some motivation in the form of an angry momma hog who wanted her babies back. I could hear my granddaddy laughing as his two grandsons ran with screaming piglets in their hands and a very large sow on their heels.

When we reached the hog pen, my cousin and I threw our piglets inside and kept on running to the safety of the barn. Their small bodies rolled into the soft mud of the pen as the sow returned to their sides, followed by the remaining piglets. Mission accomplished!

My grandfather emerged from the edge of the woods, chuckled, and confirmed what I'd figured out: "Now boys, **that** is how it's done."

After a good laugh, Granddaddy took my cousin and me down to Cooper's Grocery Store, the local hotspot where all the men of the community gathered to share their stories and farming advice. At Cooper's, we each received an ice-cold Pepsi® and a pack of peanut-butter crackers. This was a big treat — fine dining for two boys working in the South Carolina heat.

As we enjoyed our drinks and crackers, my grandfather told the story of his heroic grandsons and their adventures with the sow and her litter. The men, sitting around on upturned soda crates, belly-laughed at the story of our great adventure. My cousin and I were the center of attention, and we loved every minute of it, especially when the men slapped us on the back as gestures of their approval.

As funny as that story is, the real value is in the life lessons I learned. I learned more than how to get a hog and her litter back into the pen. That day I learned about teamwork, thinking outside of the box, the value of leadership — and the importance of praise and encouragement from an adult in the life of a boy.

In Scouting, as we train youth for life, some lessons are better learned outside of the classroom. In fact, my grandfather used his farm as a classroom to teach me many life skills that I use to this day, lessons that I now pass on to others. Looking back, I see the great value and the vision that he had for my life. Who said that learning had to be dull?

A Game with a Purpose

Scouting is learning the fun way (minus a hog chasing you). Some say that Scouting is a game with a purpose. My experiences in Scouting were fun, and that was what kept me coming back for more learning. At the same time, I learned values that would remain with me for a lifetime.

As a young Cub Scout, I sat around a small table at Mrs. Dot Godfrey's house working on projects and building Pinewood Derby cars with my dad. As I matured and moved into the Boy Scouts, I earned over fifty merit badges. I learned to fire shotguns with a South Carolina Wildlife Officer, took a fingerprinting class from a police officer, and toured the airport control tower at the Columbia Metropolitan Airport. Through all of these activities, I gained skills and knowledge that continue to help me in my adult life.

I would like to share an old story that illustrates the heart of Scouting in America:

> Two farmers lived next to each other. Each had two sons who helped to raise his crops. The first farmer worked his boys hard, but they were always laughing and having fun while they worked. The first farmer always had chores for his boys to do, so they had little time to run off with the neighboring boys.
>
> The second farmer did not work his boys as hard and let them go anytime they wanted to goof off with friends, even though they often got into trouble. The second farmer looked down on the first farmer's approach; in fact, he thought that the first farmer should not work his boys so hard to raise his crops. He would often tell the first farmer, "They're young, give them time to

grow up and have fun."

One day the two farmers were at the feed store. The second farmer watched as the first farmer's sons loaded the truck with supplies. Feeling like he should say something, the second farmer said to the first, "You know you don't have to work your boys so hard to raise your crops."

To which the first farmer replied, "You're right, but I'm not trying to raise a crop, I'm trying to raise boys into men with character and values!"

For the Good of the Cause

The aim of Scouting is to raise boys into honorable men — men who are not afraid of hard work, who have confidence in their abilities, who believe in helping others at all times, and who are men of strong character and values. Dr. Jay Strack, Student Leadership University President/CEO, says, "There comes a time in each boy's life when it is time for the boy to sit down and the man to stand up."

* * *

The closing of a Scout meeting is a brief but inspirational moment. Often the Scoutmaster will review upcoming events, share an inspirational quote, or maybe talk about the history of Scouting, before ending with a benediction. Years ago, I heard a leader conclude with, "Before we close in prayer, is there anything else for the good of the cause?"

For the Good of the Cause. That phrase has stayed with me since that time. When we close out a Scouting meeting, it's not the ending, but the time for us to live out the values of Scouting. As I close out each chapter of this book, I will end it with a challenge for you to live out and pass along the values of Scouting, "for the good of the cause."

On matters of style, swim with the current;
on matters of principle, stand like a rock.

~ *Thomas Jefferson*

The art of governing consists simply of being honest,
exercising common sense, following principle,
and doing what is right and just.

~ *Thomas Jefferson*

I love the man that can smile in trouble,
that can gather strength from distress,
and grow brave by reflection.
Tis the business of little minds to shrink,
but he whose heart is firm,
and whose conscience approves his conduct,
will pursue his principles unto death.

~ *Thomas Paine*

CHAPTER 2

SCOUTING WORKS!

What makes the Boy Scouts of America one of the most successful youth organizations in the world? There are many reasons, but one of the strongest is that Scouting teaches with a hands-on approach. Benjamin Franklin said, "Tell me and I forget. Teach me and I remember. Involve me and I learn." Scouting involves the boys in teachable situations and provides experiences that many carry with them into adulthood. Often Scouts choose their profession based on the skills they have learned while earning a merit badge or by working on their Eagle Scout project.

Such is true with Mike Rowe of the Discovery Channel's hit show, *Dirty Jobs*.

Mike's Eagle Scout project was reading to blind students. Rowe posted in an online forum, "I read and volunteered at the Maryland School for the Blind. It was, ironically, the first time I had read anything out loud and one of the reasons I became interested in narrating." (The Discovery Channel, Dirty Jobs fan website, posted March 6, 2007)

The more a Scout learns, the more a Scout earns on his Scouting journey. This can come in the form of merit badges (there were 121 merit badges as of 2009), rank advancements, and Eagle Scout projects. If a Scout works hard and earns the rank of Eagle Scout, his skill level and his knowledge base are extensive. That is the main reason so many companies and all branches of the United States military seek out Eagle Scouts to join their corporate or armed service ranks in key leadership positions.

When Eagle Scouts sign up with a branch of the military, they receive the rank of E-2 or E-3. As an example, if a Scout joins the Marine Corp and successfully completes boot camp, he will come out as a Lance Corporal, thus earning more money and having more leadership responsibility than his peers will.

Dr. George Jones: Scouting and the Military

Dr. George Jones of the Blue Ridge Mountains Council in Virginia is an Eagle Scout and serves as the Reservation Chaplain for the Council at camps Powhatan, Ottari, and Claytor Lake Aquatics Base. He shares his story of entering the military as an Eagle Scout.

> After earning my Eagle, along with several palms, I graduated from high school and went directly into the United States Air Force. I soon found out that Scouting prepared me for my military service. On the morning that the inductees arrived at boot camp in Texas, the Drill Instructor boarded the bus shouting words that I had never heard. I'll have to admit, I didn't know the human voice could actually speak such words, and having lived a sheltered life, trust me, they were all new to me.
>
> He asked if there were any Boy Scouts on the bus. None of us

said anything because we were all terrified of the man. The Drill Instructor then asked if there was an Eagle Scout on the bus. I got my nerve up to admit to that, because I was proud to be an Eagle Scout. I held up my hand and he strung off another group of expletives, and shouted out, "All right men, we've got a live one here!" He pointed to me, and said, "Gentleman, this is your new dorm chief."

Immediately I found out that Scouting was something that not only prepared me in many ways, but also was recognized by others. Even my Drill Instructor felt that an Eagle Scout, or a Scout of any rank, was someone of great character and benefit to the unit.

No Need to Worry

I never was one who took tests well in school. From elementary school to college, I had to study hard to make a decent grade. In high school, I was mostly a C student, but in college, I pushed myself to the limits to earn Bs. One semester I tried my best to make the Dean's list, only to fall short by a few tenths of a percentage. I recall how devastating that was, and how my wife congratulated me on what I had indeed accomplished. With her encouragement, I refocused, accepted my best, and completed my four-year degree in three and one-half years with a B average.

That may not sound like much, but I started elementary school with a speech impediment. I felt like I was always behind the curve in learning and I graduated high school truly not knowing the difference between a subject and predicate.

Today I speak before thousands each year and have written several books. This is possible because of the encouragement of many people. As a youth, I gained confidence from my experiences in Scouting; as an adult, I gained inspiration from my spouse, friends, and accountability partners.

Bob Kornegay: Philmont Transformation

Bob Kornegay, Unit Commissioner of the Catawba District in the Blue Ridge Mountains Council (Virginia), shared this Scouting story about inspiring others to greatness:

> In 1988, I took the first of my seven trips to Philmont Scout Ranch near Cimarron, New Mexico. My contingency also included Scouter Hal Cantrel and ten Scouts, all from the Blue Ridge Mountains Council.
>
> Things went smoothly prior to the trip, with several shakedown weekends on the Appalachian Trail to get our group on the same page. However, once we were on the trail at Philmont, a serious problem arose. One of the Scouts was not carrying his weight. He ignored duty rosters, and had an all-round bad attitude.
>
> Other members of the crew wanted to dump him before we were too far down the trail. This type of behavior doesn't cut it at Philmont. Hal and I needed to talk with this young man so our group could get back on track.
>
> It turned out that this Scout was quite a classical musician and played in the local Youth Symphony. However, he thought that his dad didn't think his interest in music was manly. This Scout had signed up for Philmont only to please his father, and was determined to hate every minute of the trek.
>
> He hadn't mentioned this prior to the trip, and his behavior

now was thoughtless and unfair to the other members of the crew. Our advice was forceful, but friendly. He could rethink the situation, take advantage of the wonderful Philmont experience, carry home great memories, and shoulder his crew responsibilities. The other option was to have the next staffed camp area radio for someone to pick him up and let him fly home.

The look on his face pretty much said it all. No way was he going to let his dad think he had failed! For the remainder of the trek, we had a changed Scout. He apologized to the crew, asked how he could make things right, and proceeded to do so. On the flight home, he was smiling, laughing, and obviously somehow different.

The November following our trek, he showed up at my place of business. At that time, I had a music store; you see, I am a musician too, so I could understand that young man's passion for music. His mom, dad, and sister were with him, and he introduced me as one of the two Scouters who helped make his Philmont trip a great experience.

His dad shook my hand and proceeded to give me tickets to the Youth Symphony Christmas concert. I still remember his exact words, "John (not the Scout's real name) still hasn't stopped talking about how great his time at Philmont was. I really wasn't sure how he would do, but it looks like I didn't need to worry. By the way, John is playing first chair in the Symphony. We're so proud of him."

Did Hal and I do something special, or was it Philmont? Perhaps a little of both ... either way, Scouting had an influence on both this Scout and his family. I lost track of John over the years, but I'll bet he's doing okay.

The Buddy System

In Scouting, there is a system to ensure that you are never alone, and when in need, you have someone by your side. This system, known by all Scouts as the Buddy System, was first put into action as a swimming safety precaution. In Baden-Powell's book, *Scouting for Boys*, the founder of the Scouting movement had this to say:

> In the Boy Scouts of America, a so-called "buddy-system" is used. The two boys of the buddy team are of about equal swimming ability. When in the water, each buddy is responsible for the safety of the other, under the general supervision of the Scouter in charge of the whole party. (1908, p. 108)

The buddy system became more than a pool safety regulation, and is foundational to the Scouting program. As a Scout, you are teamed up with a buddy before you hit the pool, head off into the woods, or spend a night camping. If a Scout asks to take a walk down the trail, the leader will respond, "Yes, you can go, but who is and where is your buddy?" Once teamed with a buddy, the Scout may then take a hike or swim.

Why is the buddy system so important? There are many reasons. One is the increased safety level when you add that second person to the situation. Survival ability is greater when there are two, and productivity increases with a set of extra hands. I have heard for most of my life that many hands make for light work. This is true when a Scout has a buddy by his side.

As a youth in Scouting, I went with my troop on one of our favorite outings, Deep Freeze Camping, at Camp Daniel Boone in North

Carolina. The goal was to camp in the coldest weather possible, at least a few degrees below zero, and if it snowed, the camping was that much better.

Cold weather and heavy snow blessed us on this particular camping trip. Our troop had USMC goose-down mummy bags that kept us toasty at night. During the daytime, we were active in sledding and building snow forts, which kept us warm.

Late one afternoon, I saw a set of rabbit tracks near our campsite. I followed the tracks — without permission and without my buddy. I didn't notice that I was getting deeper into the woods and away from camp. After about thirty minutes of trekking, I realized that the sun was about to drop behind the face of the mountain.

The beauty of the moment faded with the glow of the sun, and with that realization, fear overcame me. The temperature was dropping. My clothing was heavy with my perspiration. That dampness and the cold would place me in serious danger — making me unable to maintain my body temperature.

I stopped to regain my bearings in the woods. Then it hit me that, as I had been tracking the rabbit by following its prints in the snow, all I needed to do was to follow my own tracks back to camp.

My heart raced with anticipation because the tracks were disappearing in the fading light. I walked quickly and I finally saw the glow of our campfire. By this time, it was dark and I was shivering. As I walked into our base camp, I found that the troop was worried about me and was about to go out to look for me.

The concerned leaders questioned me about my absence, but they were relieved that I was okay. Then I became the object lesson for the rest of the troop, "Gentlemen," the Scoutmaster stated, "this is why you need to practice the buddy system!" I didn't mind being an example because I was thankful to be standing by the warm campfire.

I have carried the Buddy System over into my adult life too. Why? As I was lost in the woods as a youth, if I am not careful I can get lost in the jungle of life as an adult.

In my book *Out of the Box and Loving It*, I wrote about the buddy system from a biblical point of view. Since 2004, I have been part of a group of six to seven guys that gets together every Thursday at 6:30 a.m. for a time of prayer and accountability. It would be impossible for me to adequately share with you what an encouragement these men have been in my life. Even if I am on the road traveling with work or with Scouts, I can always count on at least one of them to call to check on me and to pray with me.

The Apostle Paul had men in his life who were a great help to him and the ministry that God had called him to. "Only Luke is with me. Bring Mark with you when you come, for he will be helpful to me" (2 Timothy 4:1). What about you? Do you have someone in your life who is helpful to you?

If you think that you are too mature or macho for a buddy system, consider the advice of Dan Carrison and Rod Walsh. In their book, *Semper Fi, Business Leadership the Marine Corps Way*, they have this to say about the buddy system:

One of the most successful Marine Corps recruiting concepts is the buddy system. Two friends who might be otherwise unprepared to readily take on the challenges of boot camp alone can enlist together with the guarantee that both will go through basic training in the same unit, and, assuming both qualify for the identical specialty (e.g. infantry, tanks, artillery), continue throughout their hitch together... It is important to note that the Marine Corps considers the buddy system to be inviolate. It is not a gimmick, but a promise that is honored. (1999, 2005, page 15)

Carrison and Walsh feel that the buddy system helps reduce turnover in the business world, and that the buddy system lends itself to a "more natural mentoring process (p. 16)" with the stronger buddy assisting the other with needed skills. Why not incorporate the buddy system into your life? If this system is good enough for the Scouts, good enough for the Marines, and good enough for corporate America, then it would be great for your life too.

For the Good of the Cause

In his book, *Be Satisfied*, Warren W. Wiersbe says, "Methods are many, principles are few, methods may change; principles never do." (1990, p. 28)

Why has Scouting stood the test of time? The main reason is that the principles of Scouting are timeless. Some may argue that Scouting is old-fashioned, archaic, and not in touch with the times, but I will argue that values, ideas, and character will never be out of style because they do not have an expiration date.

Leadership is unlocking people's potential to become better.

~ *Bill Bradley*

In order to be a leader a man must have followers. And to have followers, a man must have their confidence. Hence, the supreme quality for a leader is unquestionably integrity. Without it, no real success is possible, no matter whether it is on a section gang, a football field, in an army, or in an office. If a man's associates find him guilty of being phony, if they find that he lacks forthright integrity, he will fail. His teachings and actions must square with each other. The first great need therefore is integrity and high purpose.

~ *Dwight D Eisenhower*

Someone I love made a difference in my life, it was my dad. He changed me because he helps me in Boy Scouts. He also taught me how to use a knife, and taught me how to set up a tent. When he spends time with me, he makes me feel loved. That's how he made a difference in my life.

~ *from a student essay, Chapel Hill Academy*

CHAPTER 3

SCOUT LEADERS MAKE A DIFFERENCE

At a Roundtable meeting, Ken Lyons, Director of Field Service for the Blue Ridge Mountains Council, thanked all of the Scout leaders for their dedication to Scouting and the commitment it takes to make a troop a successful unit. He said, "You have to be a great business leader to run a troop; it's much like running a small business. You have to develop plans, organize, fill out paperwork, and manage your budget. In some ways you do more than a small business owner, so thank-you for all you do!"

Scout leaders are dedicated people with skills to lead. I had only three Scout leaders as a youth. In Cub Scouts, there was Mrs. Dot Godfrey. Even to this day, when I visit my hometown in South Carolina I have the opportunity to visit with Mrs. Godfrey and fondly remember the times in her home working on projects and learning as a young Cub Scout.

As I moved up to the troop level, I was blessed by the experience and dedication of Mr. Virley Seay. As you will learn more about him and his amazing life later in this book, Mr. Seay was a man who had a deep dedication to his Scout troop and was the founder of our unit. Finally, there was my dad, M.B. Shaw, who had a vision and an influential way of training young men to become true leaders. As I write this book, my dad is in his eighties, and still works hard in Scouting.

Our troop was and still is much like a family. For over four generations now, my Scoutmaster dad has worked with and trained Scouts on a troop, district, and council level. When my mom passed away in November of 2008, there were so many Scouts at the funeral that it was truly a comfort to our family.

Roland Young: Scouting with Mr. M.B. Shaw

Recently I spoke with my friend Roland Young. He and I grew up together and were in Scouting together. This is what Roland had to say about his troop and his Scoutmaster, M.B. Shaw:

> The river of life has been a violent current for me, and has nearly washed me down stream. Working to pay bills, raising a child, and dealing with health problems have affected me.
>
> But, I can say without reservation that I carry my experiences in Boy Scouts with me every day of my life. I was lucky to be in a Boy Scout troop led by Mr. M.B. Shaw. His entire family was involved in Troop 424. His incredible wife, Vera, was like a second mother to me, and Mr. Shaw was like a father to me. His son, Todd, was like my brother.
>
> My Scouting experience touched my entire life. The lessons and examples, set by my Scoutmaster and his wife, of love, patience, God, and country, have served me well.
>
> As a man, I share the character that Scouting developed in me

with others every day. Not only did I personally benefit from Scouting, but everyone who meets me also benefits. Scouting is like dropping a pebble in calm water and watching the ripples move out further and further from the pebble. My Scoutmaster, M.B. Shaw, was my pebble. Not only did the experience nurture character, it was a blast. Those were some of the happiest times of my life.

I don't know about you but that brings a tear to my eyes every time I read that story from Roland, not because he's writing about my dad, but because the heartfelt impact that a dedicated Scoutmaster had still plays out each day of his life.

The same story is being replicated as Scout leaders attend leader training, and then use that knowledge to plan and carry out troop meetings every week. They give freely of their time with one goal in mind: to have an impact on a young man's life through Scouting. Rewind to the year 1910 and imagine the stories that could be told. They would no doubt fill volumes of books with stories that still ripple out, further and further from the pebble — the Scout leader.

Involved Fathers

In high school, I was riding around with some non-Scouting buddies. They shared stories and complained that their dads never did anything with them, and never talked with them.

I'm not sure why, perhaps it's our human nature, but I felt like I needed to join in on this pity party. I started sharing my woes of life and how bad that I had it in my home. I'll never forget the way my friends looked at me.

"What is it?" I asked.

"Todd, you have got to be kidding us! You have the best dad in the world. He's at all of your band events, he watches most of your soccer games, and for goodness sakes, he's your Scoutmaster. Just look at all the cool stuff that you guys get to do in the Boy Scouts. Our dads won't even take the time to bring us to the meeting, but your dad takes his time to run the troop."

They were right, and I knew it. They truly had a right to complain, but I did not. I have to say that my dad set the bar high when it came to living life as a positive role model. He was an example to others.

It's funny how life moves in a circle, now I am a Scout leader and I look for and expect things to be done with the same high standard that my dad, my Scoutmaster, did things.

Not too many years ago, I attended a Court of Honor. This is where Scouts receive merit badges, rank advancements, and recognition for their accomplishments. The event was poorly executed. The leaders arrived late, they were not prepared, and they didn't have all the awards that the Scouts had earned. I wondered why they wasted their time in Scouting.

The next day my dad called to see how the event turned out. I told him about the evening and the disappointment that I saw on the faces of the young Scouts when the awards they had earned were not presented to them.

Then it hit me. I said, "You know whose fault it is?"

"No, whose?" my dad replied.

"It's all your fault. Yes sir, it's all your fault."

There was a moment of silence on the phone, and then Dad asked, "How is it my fault when I wasn't even there?"

I told him that when I was a Scout, our Court of Honor programs were major events. Families turned out in large numbers, dads who never showed up for sporting events were there to see their sons receive a rank advancement. A Court of Honor was a big deal.

"So that is why it's your fault. I've come to expect other Scout leaders to put forth that same effort that you did for us." With tears in my eyes, I said, "Thank-you, Daddy, for all that you did for us in Scouting."

Today, as I visit with my dad at his home full of Scouting memorabilia and awards, it's a common sight to see photographs of Scouts, now grown, with their families. These men send my dad pictures of their children in their Tiger Cub and Scouting uniforms and notes that thank him for having an impact on their lives.

Young men need a strong male role model in their lives; it is crucial for their development and shapes who they will become. In a 1999 study by the National Center on Addiction and Substance Abuse at Columbia University, researchers looked at the relationships between teens and their parents and drug use. In an accompanying statement to the study report, the center's president, Joseph A. Califano Jr., wrote this about the father/teen relationship:

Underscoring the importance of an engaged father in a two-parent family, the CASA survey found that a child in a two-parent family with a poor or fair relationship with the father is at more than 60% higher risk of substance abuse than a child growing up in a home headed by a single mother who has an excellent relationship with that mother. About 35% of single mother households surveyed fit this description.

This should be a wake-up call for dads across America. Every father should look in the mirror and ask: "How often do I eat meals with my children? Take them to religious services? Help with their homework? Attend their games and extracurricular activities? Join mom in monitoring my teen's conduct, praising and disciplining them? (Califano 1999)

Noted psychologist Dr. James Dobson also speaks and writes about the impact of uninvolved fathers. Here is what he shared on his Focus on the Family website about Fathers' Day in prison:

Some years ago, executives of a greeting card company decided to do something special for Mother's Day. They set up a table in a federal prison inviting any inmate who so desired to send a free card to his mom. The lines were so long, they had to make another trip to the factory to get more cards. Due to the success of the event, they decided to do the same thing on Father's Day, but this time no one came. Not one prisoner felt the need to send a card to his dad. Many had no idea who their fathers even were.

Don Miers: The Influence of Mr. John Collins

Boys need a father who is a good role model for them, and sometimes a Scoutmaster is the only father figure a boy may have.

That was the case for former Detroit Tigers Executive, Don Miers:

> I was raised without a father. The first and foremost person who helped me become a leader is my mother, Stella. She did it by example. She had an incredible work ethic that I have not seen in any other human being. We lived in the northern New Jersey suburbs of New York City, and we didn't own a car until I was in high school. My mother commuted via bus, train, and subway to work — a two-hour trip to New York. She was never late for work. She never called in sick. She never took a day off. She worked in the international banking business on Wall Street, beginning as a bank teller and working her way up to a vice president.
>
> Because I was an only child without an adult male influence, my mother and I thought the Boy Scouts of America would be good for me. It certainly was, largely because of the influence of my Scoutmaster, Mr. John Collins. He was a true leader, and he taught and trained his Scouts to be leaders as well. He got involved with his Scouts, showing us, hands-on, how to do things. As a leader with authority, he was firm, yet fair. If there was a problem or disagreement, he would listen to both sides before making a decision.
>
> Mr. Collins was a great role model — not only a leadership example but also a great model of people skills. During the four years that he was such a big part of my life, he was always available to talk when I needed advice or someone to talk with.
>
> When I was sixteen, Mr. Collins died of cancer. I miss him to this day. (Excerpted from Pat William's, *Coaching Your Kids to be Leaders*. Reprinted by permission.)

John C. Matthews: My Scoutmaster and Friend, Mr. Virley Seay

John C. Matthews spent his days in Scout Troop 343 in West Columbia, South Carolina. Here is his story of the impact that one Scout leader had on his life.

I was a Cub Scout and my mom was my Den Leader. Like most moms, she made a natural role model for the younger Scouts. She helped pave the way for learning how to do the right thing the right way.

Advancing onward and upward, Boy Scouts taught me how to do things for myself. Using my imagination while working on merit badges and building projects for the Camporees really improved my skills.

During the summer of 1964, when I was fourteen, I joined a Scout troop across town. Mr. Seay was our Scoutmaster and we met in his barn for many years. That was where I could fit in. That was where I first met Mr. Virley Seay, and he became my role model as the years went by. The troop was like a family, so much so that the older Scouts called Mr. Seay "Uncle Bub."

I excelled in and obtained more merit badges than I thought possible but my time ran out because of my age and I didn't make Eagle. That was quite a blow to me. I can still remember Mr. Seay taking me aside, consoling me, and explaining the reason I couldn't make my goal, Eagle. I'm not sure what happened next, but I know I didn't give up!

At that point, Mr. Seay started an Explorer Scout program with those of us ready to advance on before we aged out of the Boy Scouting program. I was the first to sign up. Mr. Seay became our Scout Advisor and even greater, he became my best friend for life. Our new Explorer Post 424 became the first Co-ed Explorer Post around the Columbia, South Carolina, area and it grew with leaps and bounds. We were all looking for something new in life and this Explorer Troop was it!

We still met in the old barn or in Mr. Seay's front living room. Phyllis, Mr. Seay's daughter, lived down the street and we eventually started meeting in her home, too. The group became more like brothers and sisters and anything we did, we did it with all of our hearts. We had many projects. We built a removable bed for a stake body truck so we could travel together on camping trips. We also built a chuck wagon to carry our kitchen equipment and food too.

Once at the campsite, all of our names were placed in a hat, drawn, and everyone shared the cooking and clean up without hesitation. I can remember one trip when the girls weren't with us, we hiked up in the trails, and someone had the idea that one of us should play like he was hurt, this way we could practice our first aid skills. One Explorer named David, being the smallest, was picked to be the victim. We made a stretcher from what we had and carried him back to the campsite. I think we almost killed him before it was all over. We didn't get back to camp until just before dusk, and Mr. Seay was starting supper. He didn't let on that he was worried; he trusted that we were all right because he knew that we would take care of each other.

As time went on, I was to go in the Navy to be stationed in Da Nang, Vietnam. Many friends and former Scouts that I had met over the years were present at a party held for me just outside the old barn. This was hard for me, because I didn't know what was ahead of me in Vietnam. Mr. Seay and his wife, Mildred, became my second parents many years prior and, well it hurt to leave and to say good-bye to them. While I was overseas, Mrs. Seay passed away, and their old house was taken down to make way for a new Scout building in her memory. Mr. Seay had moved down the street to his daughter Phyllis's house.

When I made it home, I was surprised to see that the foundation of the new Scout hut was just complete. Many Scouts and former Scouts participated in the construction process. The building was finally finished and used for many more years. It was filled with Cub and Boy Scouts, but the Explorer Scouts started falling off.

Explorer Post 424 was fading away, that was our generation of Explorer Scouts, and I will forever remember them as one of a kind. We didn't recognize it at the time, but we were being groomed for patience and skills. Mr. Seay saw something in us that we didn't see in ourselves. He took a chance with us, one that changed our outlook on life and definitely shaped our future.

I even met Susan, my wife, through our Explorer Post. When it came time for our wedding, there was only one choice, only one person who could stand beside me on such a special day. I asked Mr. Virley Seay to be my best man. He accepted and that's all that mattered. Susan and I eventually bought land from Mr. Seay. He, along with family, friends, and my generation of Explorer Scouts, built our home in 1972.

Mr. Virley Seay was a father figure to all of us, a man of his own right, a friend for life, and then some. Most of all he was a true leader and role model. He was one who instilled values, the meaning of a handshake, and a witness for our Lord throughout his life. And to me, he was my best man. Yes, I miss him, we all do. He took us in, and I will ever be grateful for the day I met him.

Today whenever Mr. Seay's name is mentioned in a conversation, you can believe it is positive and brings back many good memories. When I heard the title of this book was to be, A Scout

Is... I thought, yes, this is Mr. Virley Seay! This is the time for a book to truly portray the lives of those who excelled in their unselfish gift to the sons and in our case, daughters too, whose lives were touched through Scouting, and who grew up to be respected citizens wherever they roamed.

For the Good of the Cause

According to the Boy Scouts of America's 2008 annual report, there were 1,165,828 adults members. That is over one million adults giving of their time and talents. For one hundred years, Scout Leaders all across this land have raised young men to become strong leaders for this nation, and they will continue doing so in the future. Thank-you!

Troop 424 - Americana Color Guard (1976)

Roland Young (center, bottom row)
S.C. Wildlife Officer teaching gun safety

Todd Shaw - Arrow of Light Award

Troop 424 - Letter of Commendation from Gerald Ford
(standing, left-right: Mike Pelletier, John Teal, Todd Shaw,
Bill Swygert; kneeling: Roe Young and Tommy Lewis)

Troop 424 - BSA Camporee at Ft. Jackson, Columbia, SC

John Matthews (bottom left) in Cub Scouts

John Matthews Troop - Gatlinburg, TN (1967)

John Matthews Troop - Camping Trip
(Virley Seay, seated on right)

Half a truth is often a great lie.

~ *Benjamin Franklin*

Save me from the fatal sword! Rescue me from the power of my enemies. Their mouths are full of lies, they swear to tell the truth, but they lie.

~ *Psalms 144:11*

Trust men and they will be true to you, treat them greatly, and they will show themselves great.

~ *Ralph Waldo Emerson*

CHAPTER 4
A SCOUT IS TRUSTWORTHY

In the first twenty-one years of my marriage, my wife and I moved thirteen times. You are probably thinking that either my wife really loves me or she really likes to move. To answer your question, yes, she really does love me and no, she really hates moving. We have finally settled down, hopefully for good, in the Blue Ridge Mountains of Virginia.

When we first left home as a young married couple, my dad gave me this piece of advice. "Todd, each time you move you'll leave behind good friends, and you'll also need to make some new ones. Your word (being truthful) is your greatest way to build life-long friends and establish a good name in a new community where no one knows you."

Bill Dial: A Man's Word is His Bond

Telling the truth is not always the easiest thing to do, especially if you think it will let a person down or if it may cost you to do so. However, there is nothing worse than being caught in a lie, so why not tell the truth from the start? If it's your boss, your spouse, a friend, or even a complete stranger, follow this advice from Eagle Scout Bill Dial:

> From my beginnings in Scouting, I have tried to tell the truth at all times and to be a trustworthy person. I have been entrusted with the responsibility of the financial health of a multi-million dollar company. I am proud of my reputation as a hard working, trustworthy person, be it in my business or personal life.
>
> I have been happily married for eighteen years. I have had four jobs my entire life. The terms of employment for the three longest tenures have been six and a half years, four years, and fifteen years. I am forty-one years old now. I have never been fired from a job. I believe that if you work hard, tell the truth, and follow through on your commitments, you will be successful in life.
>
> Years after I had moved away from West Columbia, my old Scoutmaster, M.B. Shaw, told me that he always knew when he asked me to handle something for him that it would be done — no matter how big or small the job. I take pride in his words to this day.
>
> I believe that a man's word is his bond and that he is only as good as his word. My parents gave me a good basis in manners and how to be polite, but my years in Scouting taught me about helping people in our community, completing service projects, teaching younger Scouts, and being an adult leader. Scouting gave me the tools and skills to be a man.
>
> When I was being considered for treasurer of our company, board members asked about my business experience and other qualifications. They were told that I am an Eagle Scout. Every male member of that board had been a Scout, and at least one was an Eagle Scout. They unanimously approved my nomination.

People trust the Scouting program because it produces fine young men like Bill Dial, a man with honor. However, a Scout doesn't grow into a trustworthy person just by reciting the Scout Oath or Law for the first time, a Scout learns to be trustworthy through the guidance and influence of adult leaders.

My Son's Dilemma

Somewhere along my journey in life, I picked up this little nugget that I have held on to tightly:

> *Tell the truth,*
> *tell it ever,*
> *cost us what it will,*
> *for he who hides the wrong he does,*
> *does the wrong thing still.*

That quote brings out a good point; it seems that we may often weigh the option to tell the truth by what it may cost us. However, a lie will cost us our reputation.

It may be tough to tell the truth, because telling the truth may prevent us from obtaining a goal or object that we have longed for and worked toward. Recently, my son was struggling with truthfulness in his own life. My little man was struggling with a character issue and needed my help. We prayed about it, talked about the importance of being a trustworthy person, and even talked about why it is important for a Scout to obey the Scout law, *A Scout is Trustworthy.*

A few weeks later, I faced a character issue too. I needed to have my medical release form signed by a doctor before I could attend Scout camp with my son and our troop. Because of my career and my heavy travel schedule, I failed to make it to the doctor and the camp date was fast approaching. Four days before camp, the document was still unsigned. I was sharing my dilemma with some others, when they expressed an easy fix to the solution: *Just make up a name of a doctor and sign it yourself, who will know?*

I am ashamed to say this, but it seemed like a harmless answer to my problem. I thought it over for a day, and then I had a talk with myself. No, I did not sign the paper, how could I? I am a Scout, an Eagle Scout. I had to get on the phone and plead with a doctor's office to give me an appointment. (Thankfully, the nurse worked me in.)

What helped me make the right decision? I weighed it out like this: I had everything to lose and nothing to gain. What type of Scout leader would I be if I were not truthful on that form? How could any young Boy Scout respect my authority as a leader if I forged that document? As an Eagle Scout, what would I be saying about the principles and character of Scouting's highest honor? As a father, how could I teach my son about the importance of being a trustworthy person, when I could not hold to that value in my own life?

A few days after this incident, my son and I were having another conversation about truthfulness, when he asked, "Dad, do you ever struggle with telling the truth?"

It seems that most kids think that adults never struggle with any issues in life. I said, "Sure, son," and I told him of my struggle with telling the truth on the medical release form, but I also told him how Scouting helped me make the correct decision.

Young or old, minute-by-minute, we face many challenges to be a fake or to be the real deal in life. Will I lie to get ahead, give a false testimony to escape the extra cost, or even exaggerate to appear greater than I am? Remember, there is never a wrong time to do the right thing.

Trustworthiness Earns Respect

I can recall from an early age the respect that my father and grandfather received from people in the community. They did not have tons of money or high prestigious positions; they earned respect with their strong and unwavering characters.

I believe that when you practice a life of strong character people will trust you with more, and from a business perspective, value you as an employee. Therefore, you will earn more, gain higher positions, and reap greater rewards. For years now, I have taught this principle to teens, and have challenged them to make the following commitments to their employer:

1. Arrive at work and be at your workstation ten minutes before your scheduled start time.

2. Do more than is expected of you. Ask for more work if things are slow. Take the initiative and look for ways to improve your

performance and bring a higher profit to the company. Do this in a way that will make you and your boss look good and not give the perception that you are looking to steal his job.

3. Be a person whose word is gold — your words should build trust, not sound like excuses.

4. Work the full day and then some — be the last one out of the door.

I had worked for my grandfather on his farm since I was six years old. When I was in high school, I applied for a job at a local taco restaurant. I was nervous and had doubts about my ability to obtain this minimum wage job, mainly because I had no restaurant experience.

Like most companies opening their doors for the first time, they started out with more people than they needed. After a short time, they evaluated the workers and threw out the "deadwood," so to speak. I was excited when I made the team. What I really recall during that trial period was that some of the workers had a lazy approach to their duties. I can still hear them saying, "I have more experience, so I know I'll get the job," but in the end they lost out because of their slothfulness. They were cut, not because of a lack of experience, but because they lacked character (hard work, integrity, and perseverance).

After I got the job, I kept up the diligent pace. This work ethic was what I'd been taught at home and in Scouting. Looking back, and from the insight of being a business owner myself, I have seen many employees work hard to get the job, then after their probation period, they stop working. What a shame. On the farm, I learned that just because you plant the seed doesn't ensure that you will produce a crop. If you want to pull in the harvest, there is still work after the first seed is planted.

I worked at that minimum wage job as if I owned the place, and I earned many raises. I enjoyed the increase in pay, which made me work even harder. The manager valued my work and wanted to keep me around so he rewarded my efforts. I had more responsibilities, and more wages for the greater responsibilities. In less than a year, the manager promoted me to shift supervisor even though I had no previous restaurant experience. Education is important and experience is a great teacher, but strong character is what puts education and experience into action. Without character, education and experience are just lines on a resume — words with no action.

Many years later, I opened my first restaurant. I recalled those days when I worked in that taco restaurant, and I wanted the same quality people that they once had for their new store. I looked for employees who seemed to have strong character over padded resumes. I learned to lean on my own observations of character rather than trusting a piece of paper. Why? Like any business owner, I had a big investment in my store, and I needed people that I could trust.

You earn trust over time. Each truthful word you speak is like interest building in a savings account. Truthfulness in the small things may not have a huge impact immediately, but over time, it will make you a trustworthy person.

Your Word is Like Gold

Can people depend on you? What a sobering question that can be, because it requires a simple yes or a shameful no answer. As a youth or an adult, we all have run into hypocritical people who simply could not be trusted. Unfortunately, it seems that the standard of trust is dropping as time goes on and if we are not careful, we will be escorted into a substandard state where a person's word has little or no meaning.

Sadly, we have seen political officials from the local, state, and even our national government fall short in the area of telling the truth. This filters down to and affects our society as a whole. The fact that a person makes a mistake is not the issue. What is upsetting is when we ignore a person's lack of character and still hold them up as an example to follow.

In Scouting, I learned many lessons about life from my Scoutmaster father. One lesson was about truthfulness in dealing with financial issues. He said that the worst thing in the world is to be walking down the street and see a man that you owe money to walking toward you with an angry look on his face. If you owe money to a man, be honest with him. If you cannot pay, go to him, don't make him hunt you down. Tell him the truth and pay when you can, but keep your word.

A group of men once approached my father and wanted him to run for a city council seat. They courted him for weeks, and were even willing to support 100 percent of his campaign. They called and visited our home many times, but in the end, my father declined to run for office.

Afterwards, I asked, "Why wouldn't you like to be on the city council and help the people of our town?"

He explained his reason in this way, "Todd, those men wanted to use me. I have a good name in this community, and I want to keep that good name for as long as I can. Those men wanted me to run so they could use me and use my name. It's not worth losing my name and integrity over a political seat."

Because my dad and Scouting instilled in me the importance of a good name, I have worked hard to protect and preserve my name wherever I go. It takes work, but you build a strong name by your actions. When I first moved to Ocala, Florida, for a new job, my family and I had to start over in a town where we knew no one. When I returned the moving truck to the rental shop, I handed the man my contract. He noticed that there was a change on the contract, one that was in my favor. He looked at it and said that he could not accept the contract as it was. When I asked why, he said, "How am I to know that you did not change this to save yourself sixty dollars?"

I said, "Sir, you do not know me, but I want you to know one thing, I would never steal sixty dollars from you because my name and reputation are worth a lot more than sixty dollars. If you would please call the location where I first picked this truck up, I'm sure the manager there can clear up this whole issue."

The man still thought that I was shooting him a line so he picked up the phone thinking that I would back down at any moment. It was our little game of poker, each man standing his ground for a sixty-dollar cash pot. The man made the call. To his amazement, the manager at the pickup location assured him that he was the one who had changed the contract and not me.

When the manager got off the phone, he looked at me and said, "Well, I guess you're right."

I thanked him for taking the time to make the call and said, "It's not about being right, it's about building trust and a good name. I was not going to walk out of here and let you think that Todd Shaw is a cheat and crook. When I leave here, I want you to think that Todd Shaw is a man of his word, someone that you can trust."

The manager looked at me and said, "You are and I do."

A Cub Scout Out Behind the Barn

Incredibly, my grandfather always had a knack for teaching and seeing the truth in others. One time I made my own cigar from the tobacco on our farm. It was the biggest, brightest, golden leaf of cured tobacco that I had ever seen. I took the huge leaf, cut all of the stems out, and used it to roll my own handmade cigar. I'm telling you, Fidel Castro would have been proud of this one. I held up the cigar and put it to my lips as if I was a Wall Street big shot with a fine Cuban cigar.

My grandfather walked by me with a big smile on his face, then stopped at the sight of me with the oversized cigar sticking out of my mouth, "Todd what are you going to do with that cigar?"

"Oh nothing Granddaddy. Ain't she a beaut?"

He smiled and said, "Sure, but you're not going to smoke that are you?

"Oh no!" I said. "This is just for looks." My grandfather knew the entire time that I planned to smoke that cigar before the sun went down.

Late in the evening, I went off behind the barn to smoke my tobacco delight. Now if you did not have the privilege of growing up on a farm, let me explain that most of the misbehaving on a farm happens behind a barn. That's where farm kids have their first drink, their first kiss, and for me, my first smoke.

As I lit the handmade cigar, I took the biggest drag I possibly could. What my grandfather knew was what I was about to learn: you cannot smoke straight tobacco. It is too hard and pure. Tobacco must first be treated and processed, toned down. The cigar was terrible! How could something so beautiful hurt my insides so badly? That had to be the closest thing to drinking rocket fuel because my mouth, lungs, and sinus cavities lit up like the lights of Disney World at Christmas.

After supper that night, Granddaddy came up to me and asked, "How was that cigar?"

I dropped my head, because I knew that he was wise to my game the entire time. "Not too good," I said. That was all the lesson that I needed.

I wasn't the only recipient of Granddaddy's insistence on truth,

A SCOUT IS...

or his grace either. One time, a worker on the farm tried to take advantage of my grandfather by stealing gas from him. I became angry over the situation, but my grandfather had a smile on his face. After the man finished painting a wonderful story all based on lies, my grandfather said, "Wouldn't you rather share the truth with me than to leave here knowing that you are living a lie?"

The man paused and said, "Mr. King, I just need some gas and I don't have the money, so I thought—"

My grandfather stopped the man and said, "Now let's start over, but this time with the truth." After that lesson on truth, my grandfather gave the man his gas, and we never had a problem with him again. In fact, he became a better and harder worker on the farm.

It didn't matter what my grandfather was doing — selling tobacco or hogs, or sawing up lumber at his mill — he was a man that you could trust. Because of his reputation, people loved doing business with him. He worked hard to make sure there was no doubt in the customers' minds that they got a fair and valuable deal.

Sometimes you can teach your kids about truth and that teaching moment will keep them out of trouble. Then there are other times that you teach your kids about truth after they have been through the fire, or in my case, the cigar. My parents and grandparents were good about loving me through the tough lessons of life, even when I had lied to them.

Because of those experiences, I try to practice that same approach when working with Scouts. Recently I was working with a Scout, helping him earn his Tenderfoot rank. We talked about the correct way to complete his project and went through the entire how-to points.

When it was time for him to demonstrate the skill, he looked at me and asked, "What, you mean I have to do it now?"

"Of course, it's your turn to show what you've learned. I already have my Tenderfoot rank."

He fumbled with the task and questioned every step because he lacked the experience and confidence. Finally, in a moment of frustration he turned to me and asked, "Aren't you here to help me?"

"Yes I am, and I did help you, but I can't do it for you. Now try again; remember what I taught you and learn from your past mistakes."

This time he moved through the project with more confidence and actually succeeded and reached his goal. He looked up with a big grin on his faced and said, "I did it and didn't need your help!" His expression was priceless. What a great lesson it is when we learn from our mistakes and go on to live a better life, which is what the Boy Scouts of America teaches young men.

Dave Durham: Scouter with No Sons of His Own

In Scouting, you will meet many exceptional and outstanding people who are committed to upstanding character. There was a man in my council that we Scouts called "Uncle Dave." Dave Durham was a full-blown character who loved Scouting and Scouts. He had more sayings than a fortune cookie factory and could always liven up a room.

The interesting thing about Uncle Dave was that he had no boys of his own. He was in Scouting because he loved it. I had the privilege of going to school with one of Dave's daughters, Elizabeth Durham. I asked Elizabeth to share a story about her dad, and she writes:

> Our dad believed in what the Boy Scouts of America represented and how it would shape future individuals. When he first went to the Boy Scouts of America to seek employment, the staff doubted his ability to perform the job due to injuries he received in WWII. He told them he would work for a year without pay to prove he had what it took.
>
> This dedication showed that he was trustworthy and could do the job. He earned the utmost respect from those who he met in more than twenty-five years of service in the Boy Scouts of America.

For the Good of the Cause

A Scout is a dependable person. He keeps his word and tells the truth. Others know they can depend on him. A Scout is guided by a higher standard: the Scout Oath and Law. His actions back up those words. Because he is a trustworthy person, he earns a good reputation. *A Scout is Trustworthy.*

A friend is one with whom you are comfortable, to whom you are loyal, through whom you are blessed, and for whom you are grateful.

~ *William Arthur Ward, author of Fountains of Faith*

I'll take fifty percent efficiency to get one hundred percent loyalty.

~ *Samuel Goldwyn, American film producer*

A boy can learn a lot from a dog: obedience, loyalty, and the importance of turning around three times before lying down.

~ *Robert Benchley, American Humorist*

CHAPTER 5

A SCOUT IS LOYAL

I love to do word studies of Latin phrases. One of my favorites is *Nihil prius fide*, which means *nothing surpasses loyalty*, or *nothing surpasses good faith*. You may see this phrase if your notary is Spanish. All Spanish notaries must abide by this official motto, which is the foundation of their profession. What an amazing code of honor to live by.

Another favorite Latin phrase that I think has a powerful meaning is *Semper Fidelis*, meaning *Always Faithful*, the motto of the United States Marine Corps. Marines have a strong code of conduct that they live by; it is ingrained in them from the first day of training.

There are strong roots of loyalty flowing out of each of those Latin phrases, words that can bring you inspiration, words that will shape your life. Being loyal means being faithful or devoted to a person or cause. Boy Scouts learn to be loyal to their troop, to their country, to their friends, and the list goes on.

Loyalty Isn't Always Convenient

This I know about loyalty: it is never convenient! Suppose you make a commitment to do something and many people are counting on you to follow through with your word and obligation. The day before the commitment, you receive an invitation to an all-expenses-paid outing. The catch to this complimentary outing is that it's on the same day as your commitment to the first group. What do you do? Well that all depends on where your loyalty lies. If your loyalty is with your commitment, you will stay true to your word and fulfill your obligation. If not, you will break your promise to the first group, and take the excursion.

I am a public speaker and am often asked to speak to youth groups. Sometimes the request may be for a large, funded event, which is able to pay me for my time and travel. Other times, requests come from smaller groups with little funding, and I may be asked to donate my time. Years ago, I decided to be loyal to my calling as a public speaker, and that included loyalty to the group that requested my time, whether they were a paying group or not.

The real test came when I committed to speak to a smaller group of teens without pay. A company that I had previously done some work for called with an invitation for my wife, Lisa, and me to go on an all expenses paid cruise to the Bahamas.

"You're kidding me!" I shouted into the phone. At first it sounded like a grand idea, I could envision us living it up on this cruise, dancing in the moon light. Then I looked at my schedule and realized that there was a conflict. I told the gentleman that

I needed to call him back. As Lisa and I discussed the situation, the answer was obvious. Within the hour, I called the company president and told him that we greatly appreciated his offer, but could not make the trip at this time. There would be no living it up, no dancing in the moon light with my lovely wife, and that was hard to accept.

I quickly had to put that thought out of my head and get ready for my speaking engagement. That Wednesday night I spoke to a group of twenty-five teens and we had a great time. It wasn't a cruise, but I knew that I made the correct decision. I can remember the excitement on the teens faces as I spoke and challenged them to live lives of greatness. On the drive home, I thought about the cost of being loyal. Being loyal is not easy, and it comes with great sacrifice at times. You must put self aside in order to fulfill your obligation to others. However, the impact can be great and shape lives for years to come.

David Smoot: Integrity and Loyalty

David Smoot, a missionary from Ocala, Florida, was in Troop 231 in Decatur, Georgia, as a Scout. He told me how the loyalty of his Scoutmaster shaped his life. David shares his story about integrity and loyalty, qualities that most people want others to believe they possess. However, many people are noticeably lacking in these qualities today. They break promises, shade the truth, and outrightly deceive others. These actions neither endear them to others, nor portray them as people of integrity. Here is David's story:

As I am quickly closing in on the sixth decade of my life, I remember that the men who led Troop 231 were people who could be counted upon to do what they said they would do. Experience has taught me that even the best intentions must be changed or cancelled sometimes because of circumstances, which cannot be overcome. And, I am sure that was the case for our troop. However, as one of the boys of 231, I never felt the sense of betrayal or abandonment because of a broken promise or a word spoken hastily that went unfulfilled. I am thankful for that positive example provided by those men. Because of them, I trust that the same can be said of me when others look back at the times we have walked together.

Jim Moore: Loyalty to God and Country

For Jim Moore, Technical Support Supervisor for Franklin Graham's Samaritan's Purse, the Scout Oath and Law are liberating words of power, words that shaped his life to be loyal to both God and Country:

My first award in Scouting was the God and Country award. My pastor encouraged me to perform all the requirements, and many of them involved local church activities related to Bible teaching, public speaking, and performing ministry-based support for the pastor.

This work eventually led me to be involved not only with my church for fifty years, but also in full time missions ministry with Samaritan's Purse.

I believe every decision I've made since my Cub Scout days was influenced by the desire to be loyal to my country and to God. I became a Marine because of that desire and served in Vietnam. I married a Christian woman with the same principles as I have. I have always sought integrity as a testimony of Christ in my life.

Anyone who has read and memorized the Scout Oath can find all twelve points somewhere in the Holy Scriptures. The founders could not have put together such an organization without faith in the one I serve.

For the Good of the Cause

When people think of loyalty, they often think of the devotion of a dog. Dogs are known to be loyal to their masters. A Scout is loyal to the principles of Scouting. Because of this loyalty, he builds strong friendships, is faithful to his country, and is steadfast to his faith. Even in the face of adversity, a Scout remains true to his family, friends, Scout leaders, school, nation, and most of all God. A Scout is Loyal.

Everybody wants to save the earth; nobody wants to help Mom do the dishes.

~ *P. J. O'Rourke*

Your rewards in life are in direct proportion to your service.

~ *Earl Nightingale*

For I was hungry, and you fed me. I was thirsty, and you gave me a drink. I was a stranger, and you invited me into your home. I was naked, and you gave me clothing. I was sick, and you cared for me. I was in prison, and you visited me.

~ *Jesus of Nazareth (Matthew 25:35-36)*

CHAPTER 6
A SCOUT IS HELPFUL

Of all the fun stuff I did in Scouting as a youth, I especially remember our troop's service projects. If a need came to my Scoutmaster dad's attention, he did something about it. Every Christmas we would deliver fruit and care baskets to the needy. He made sure that we didn't just drop off the baskets and say God bless and good-bye in the same breath. He showed us how to talk and listen to the people that we were visiting. As we got older, he would step back and let us boys do all the talking.

Bill McCutcheon: Helping and Caring

Bill McCutcheon, fellow Eagle Scout, and President/CEO of the American Kart Racing Association, shared a similar story with me about his days in Scouting with BSA Troop 899 in Conway, South Carolina.

> As a Scout, I learned the delight of being of service and helpful to those I came in contact with on a daily basis. That same approach has helped me find success in my personal growth and success in my business life as well.

When I was in high school, I delivered Christmas dinners to shut-ins and the elderly for my mother. To see the excitement on their faces and the gleam in their eyes that someone had taken the time to share a simple gift was priceless. I actually think I received a bigger blessing from this experience than they did.

Helping and caring for others is one of the most valuable lessons I learned in my Scouting journey.

Richard M. Marano: "Uncle Dick" Giacin Was More Than a Santa

I loved earning merit badges and skill awards when I was a Scout. If I had a goal, then I set my mind to completing a project. However, not all things in life come with rewards, payment, or accolades; there are times when it's just a good thing to be helpful. Richard M. Marano, Eagle Scout, Superior Court Judge in the State of Connecticut, and currently the president of Housatonic Council, shares a story about his time in Troop 39, in Waterbury, Connecticut.

When I was a Boy Scout, I had the privilege of knowing Richard J. Giacin Sr., or "Uncle Dick," as we called him. Uncle Dick looked just like Santa Claus. He had snow-white hair and a long white beard and played the part of Santa throughout the year. Whenever a child would approach him in hypnotic awe, Dick would never disappoint. He would play the part brilliantly and send the child away elated!

Uncle Dick was my troop's Assistant Scoutmaster, and he volunteered at Camp Mattatuck during the summer. Although he was usually seen helping park cars or making toast for breakfast, jobs that had little appeal to most Scouters, his main task was to spend time with the homesick Scouts and make them forget that they were homesick. It seemed that he always succeeded. He often took boys out on the lake fishing, and made them promise not to tell his secret fishing spots to anyone.

Dick Giacin had the closest resemblance to a Baden-Powell or an Uncle Dan Beard than anyone else I have ever met in Scouting. He knew the outdoor skills. He could tie every knot, and tie them faster than anyone else. His Navy training served him well. In addition, he made dozens of toy puzzles, which kept Scouts entertained for hours.

Uncle Dick's greatest gift to me, however, was a saying that he repeated dozens of times, usually when boys were arguing over something. "Fellas," he said, "it's nice to be important, but it's important to be nice." What a great slogan!

Dick Giacin never sought accolades or awards. In fact, he shunned the spotlight. However, he did receive recognition. His humanitarian service was legendary, not only in Scouting, but throughout the City of Waterbury.

Uncle Dick's words have guided me well in life: "It's nice to be important, but it's important to be nice." He was a shining example of the third point of the Scout Law: *A Scout is Helpful.*

Roderick Kohl: Ready to Respond on the Job

A Scout must be prepared and ready to respond immediately to any situation, because he never knows what may arise. While on his summer job, Eagle Scout Roderick Kohl of Oklahoma had to respond by helping a fellow co-worker.

I was seventeen years old and had been an Eagle Scout for about a year and a half. I was operating my ride at an amusement park when a co-worker approached the outer fence of my area, said that he didn't feel well, and then fainted. I notified the park emergency team, secured my ride and its passengers, and scaled a four-foot fence to help the fallen co-worker. After surveying the area for further damage, I gave first aid to the co-worker. I immediately began to treat him for dehydration by cooling him down.

The emergency service arrived and took over from there. Without the skills and bravery that I learned through Scouting, I am not sure I would have been brave enough to handle the situation. Instead of freezing up and possibly making things worse, I was able to properly analyze the situation and respond accordingly. My focus was to help the fallen co-worker and to protect the park guests. I'm glad I was there to help!

I'd Better Take Over Now

I must admit that I love a good television commercial. Not too long ago, Holiday Inn Express ran an entertaining series. One of the spots featured a surgeon performing a risky surgery. When the operating room staff realized that the man was not the renowned surgeon, they exclaimed, "You're not Doctor Smith!"

The confident but untrained impostor responds with, "No I'm not a doctor, but I did stay at a Holiday Inn Express last night."

I read an article on Crosswalk.com about noted brain surgeon, Dr. Bronson Ray. One day he was taking a stroll when he saw a boy on a scooter smash headfirst into a tree. Realizing that the boy was seriously injured, the doctor told a bystander to call an ambulance. As he proceeded to administer first aid, a boy not much older than the injured one nudged through the crowd that had gathered and said to Dr. Ray, "I'd better take over now, sir. I'm a Boy Scout and I know first aid."

Once again, here is another one of those stories that seems to pop up about the helpfulness of an eager Scout ready to serve someone in need. Why do so many Boy Scouts respond in this way?

It's not hard to see why when you look at the top five merit badges that Scouts earned in 2008. According to the national office of the Boy Scouts of America, the top five badges and number earned by Scouts are as follow:

First Aid	84,419
Swimming	75,568
Environmental Science	72,150
Citizenship in the World	60,582
Camping	58,654

Paul Bragg II: Scouting's Influence on My Career

First Aid is a hands-on, practical part of a Scout's training. It's no wonder that so many Scouts choose a career in the medical field, from a doctor to an EMT. Here is Paul Bragg's story:

I have only been out of Scouting for maybe four years since I started Cub Scouts in the second grade. Through my experience in Scouting, I have learned and lived the Scout Law.

Scouting instilled in me the motivation for service to others and self-sacrifice. I am still involved in Scouting, and in my non-scouting life, I am a paramedic, certified peace officer, volunteer firefighter, and station chief.

I try to instill in my troop that the Scout Law is not something we recite before every meeting, but a way to live your life.

For the Good of the Cause

When it comes to being helpful I guess the great American humorist, Will Rogers, said it best, "The trouble with Boy Scouts... there ain't enough of 'em." A Scout cares about other people. He willingly volunteers to help others without expecting payment or reward. He is a true servant looking for ways to fulfill the Scout slogan, "Do a good turn daily." *A Scout is Helpful.*

If you go looking for a friend, you're going to find they're very scarce. If you go out to be a friend, you'll find them everywhere.

~ *Zig Ziglar*

Don't wait for people to be friendly. Show 'em how.

~ *unknown*

Lead the life that will make you kindly and friendly to everyone about you, and you will be surprised what a happy life you will lead.

~ *Charles M. Schwab*

CHAPTER 7

A SCOUT IS FRIENDLY

I've noticed that people hesitate when it comes to making new friends. They may be quick with the casual niceties as they pass by, but they do not readily engage in sociable conversation that leads to a true friendship.

With all of the moves my wife and I made, we had to make new friends, gain the trust of new neighbors, and get to know local merchants all over again. We had two choices: wait for people to reach out to us, or put on a smile and reach out to them. The first option is reactive and often slow moving; the second is proactive and much more rewarding.

A Brother to Every Other Scout

In Scouting, I have learned that if you want a friend you must first become a friend; after all, a Scout is friendly. A smile is the first step in being friendly. Not a fake photo-smile, but a friendly smile that tells people that you can be trusted and that you can be a true friend.

The Second Class Scout badge is a scroll with the Scout motto "Be Prepared" appearing on it. The ends of the scroll are turned up like the corners of a Scout's mouth in a smile. Sometimes we all need a reminder to smile, even in the tough times.

Today, the fourth point of the law states that *A Scout is Friendly*; however, Master Scout Robert Baden-Powell went into more detail in the original Scout Law. He wrote, "A Scout is a true friend to all and a brother to every other Scout."

When I wore my Scout uniform as a youth, my classmates would often make fun of me. I was and am proud of my Scouting heritage, but I don't think there is anyone who enjoys harassment. Even as an adult, while I am in uniform, people will walk by and give me a fake salute as a form of jest. I had a gentleman tell me that it takes a secure man to go out into public dressed like that. In all those cases, I remember that *A Scout is Friendly*, and respond in kindness. That is where character training in my youth has paid off and has shaped my conduct.

In 1967, the 12th World Scout Jamboree was held in Farragut State Park, Idaho. All 12,011 participants from 105 countries were encouraged to live up to the fourth tenet of the Scout Law. The Jamboree theme was "For Friendship."

Why is there a great need for friendship? Life can be cruel for those who may be different. A person's race, social status, or even disability can cause the unkind or ignorant person to make comments that hurt others. I have personally experienced and witnessed this on many levels. My grandfather Shaw (who died before I was born) and two of his brothers were blind. Since birth, my dad's Uncle Bud had only known the world of darkness. However, using the Braille code, Uncle Bud was an avid reader and he was a smart man.

Uncle Bud lived out his final years of life with our family. He and I shared many laughs; he was easily tickled and responded with an amazing chuckle. One time my father took Uncle Bud to a new doctor for a checkup. During the physical examination the doctor screamed, "Mr. Shaw, does this hurt?"

After this occurred several times, Uncle Bud turned to my father and said, "Tell this fool I'm blind and not deaf." Dad and my Uncle Bud broke out in laughter as the poor doctor blushed in embarrassment.

Eddie Albert: Seeing Past Labels

True friends understand that they may have differences, but they choose to focus on the friendship instead. As a Scout, Eddie Albert experienced a similar situation in his Scout troop. Here is Eddie's story:

> I had a friend in Scouts in Columbia who was different from me. And of course, young boys tend to be rather brutal towards others who are different. But this guy was fun to be with and we soon forgot what differences there were. I played basketball with him, and he was better than I was.
>
> He had two fingers on one hand, and only one leg. I learned from him that what some people consider a handicap is simply a label

we put on people.

The most memorable moment happened at a camp-out. We were running down a hill to jump in a pond to go swimming. He was beside me running, when he reached down, popped a belt loose on his prosthetic leg — allowing it to fall away — and kept right on without seeming to break stride. Right into the water we went.

I learned many things in Scouts, but the lesson of acceptance I learned that day is one that has really stuck with me.

One of the greatest lessons that you can learn is the fact that everyone has something to offer. Life is short, and it is best to go through life with your friends and a smile on your face.

Dave Durham: A Friend Can Turn a Day Around

As a Scout, I learned the great importance of being friendly. Now I don't know about you, but there are days that I don't feel like smiling or being around people. I may be tired or feeling a little down, but I push myself to call an old friend that I have not spoken to in a while. Soon, we are both laughing and having the time of our lives. A friend can turn a day around.

Dave Durham brightened the days of many Scouts by showing them friendship. Dave's daughter Elizabeth shares another story about her dad, Uncle Dave Durham.

Our dad never met a stranger. Once you met him, you were a friend for life. He always had a kind word for any individual, no matter what their status in life. Once dad retired from professional Boy Scouts, he worked each summer at Scout Camp. Scouters would flock to the trading post to find "Uncle Dave" and see what words of wisdom he would dispense to them. Scouts would drop by if they were missing home, and Dad offered his time and heart to everyone.

For the Good of the Cause

A Scout is a friend to all. He is a brother to other Scouts. He offers his friendship to people of all races and nations, and respects them even if their beliefs and customs are different from his own. A Scout is considerate of his friends. He respects them and stands up for them. A friend may bring a gift to your party, but a true friend helps you clean up after all the others have gone home. A Scout is a true friend. *A Scout is Friendly.*

A brave heart and a courteous tongue, they shall carry thee far.

~ *Rudyard Kipling, Novelist*

No one is too big to be courteous, but some are too little.

~ *unknown*

It is difficult to find a courteous person today who isn't trying to sell you something.

~ *unknown*

He who sows courtesy reaps friendship, and he who plants kindness gathers love.

~ *St. Basil*

CHAPTER 8
A SCOUT IS COURTEOUS

The Scout slogan teaches that a Scout should do a good turn daily. A good turn is a courtesy extended to others. It doesn't take much time from our day to open doors for people, help a neighbor in need, give directions to a stranger, be on time for a meeting, let a driver in during heavy traffic, be a good listener, or even say *please* and *thank-you*. When we practice courtesy, people will remember us in a positive way.

Ole Darlene

I travel a good bit and I do enjoy it; traveling is part of my life and career. The downside of so much travel is that motel rooms can get old and I can never remember the color of my latest rental car. At times, I have to walk through the parking lot pressing the panic button on the key ring so I can hear the horn honking and spot the lights flashing to locate my car.

When I travel, I love to drink coffee. Morning, noon, or night, I like a fresh cup of Joe, especially if I am driving. Once when I was in South Florida, on my way to a speaking engagement, I stopped to get some gas.

After I filled my tank, I walked into the not-so-busy store where the woman behind the counter didn't even look at me. I went to the hot drink section, grabbed a pot of coffee, and started to pour. With my cup nearly filled to the brim, I added my two sugars and two half-and-half creamers. Now here is a tip for you: if you ever want to know if the coffee is fresh, pour the half-and-half into the coffee and it should turn a nice pecan brown color. If it doesn't, then you have some old, nasty coffee on your hands, which is not fit for human consumption. The coffee I poured was more like 10W-30 motor oil, good lubricant, but not so good coffee.

I looked at the young woman who was still sitting behind the counter doing nothing. "Ma'am, do you think I could get a fresh pot of coffee?" It was a bold move, but I was willing to take a chance.

She looked up from her paper with a look that could kill and shouted in a demon-crazed voice, "What? You want me to make a fresh pot of coffee for everyone who walks through the door?"

Okay, I thought, *Step away from the coffee and nobody will get hurt.* I eased my way to the door, sidestepping the front counter where this lady was poised, ready to pounce on me like an angry mountain lioness protecting her young. I made it safely out the door, bolted to my car, and drove down the street to where someone was actually glad to have a customer.

Fast forward a few months to an almost exact situation. This time I was driving up I-75 in Georgia. I stopped in the small town of

Tifton. I pulled into a Texaco station to fill up my car. I hopped out, swiped my card, started pumping my gas, and walked into the not-so-busy store where a woman was standing behind the counter talking on the phone. Sound familiar?

I grabbed a pot of coffee and started to pour, but this time seeing only a small amount of coffee "cooking" in the bottom, I put the pot back down. Standing there looking at another pot of motor oil I thought, *Why me, Lord? Don't I live a good life? Can't I get a fresh pot of coffee? Is that too much to ask for?*

Then I heard a voice from above, an angelic voice, calling out to me in a Georgia twang, "Sugar?" I turned to see where the voice was coming from; it wasn't from heaven, but from the girl behind the counter.

Standing there, hands on her hips and waxing on chewing gum like it was the last piece in the world, the girl had a big smile on her face waiting for me to answer. I asked, "Excuse me?" I thought, *How am I to know that this isn't a trap?* The wounds from my last encounter in South Florida were still fresh. I proceeded with caution.

Then she said the words that I longed to hear, "Sugar, you want me to make you a fresh pot of coffee?"

Still unsure of the situation I asked meekly, "Would you?"

Her face lit up like a kid seeing Santa Claus coming down Main Street in a Christmas parade. "I would love to fix you a fresh pot. Now sit down right there and ole Darlene will take care of you."

Ole Darlene sashayed from behind the counter. She was on a mission. She smiled, still chewing her gum with great vigor as she went about her mission of mercy to make me — me, of all people — a fresh pot of coffee. Soon I was on my way with fresh coffee for my travels and a renewed belief in the hopes that there are still places where you can get good courteous service.

The amazing thing about that story is that I can't tell you the name of the store in South Florida — but I will never forget the negative way I was treated there. Now, the place where I got the great service was a Texaco station right off I-75 going North on the West side of the interstate in Tifton, Georgia. My memories of Darlene are different, and I'd be sure to stop in if I was ever in Tifton again. Why is that so? Because ole Darlene gave me great service and she was courteous!

Catching Flies

Courtesy can be taught or caught. Being courteous is contagious. Eagle Scout Bill Dial says:

> You catch more flies with honey than vinegar.... old saying, but true. I have tried to teach my son, who is currently a First Class Scout with Troop 84 in Anderson, South Carolina, that being polite to other people and using proper manners will take him far in life. Consider the alternative of being rude and obnoxious— which person would you rather be around?

Lisa Shaw: A Word from the Wife

I was traveling back home when I got this phone call from my wife: "Honey, your editor said she would like to have one more story on *A Scout is Courteous* for your book. What if I write a story about how I married a Scout?"

"Ahh, well um." Hey guys, how in the world do you answer that question and keep your marriage healthy? My wife is a great writer, but what in the world would she write about me as a husband? "Sure give it a shot." I said, with a little reservation in my voice.

Making my way down the road, I started to think about her assignment. I'd never thought about how Scouting has shaped me to be a better husband. I can see how Scouting helps me with social formalities or manners extended to people outside of my family, but what about to my family?

Then I realized that being courteous is fundamental in any relationship, especially in marriage. Here is Lisa's story:

> When I began dating my husband, I quickly realized the standards in his family were quite high. I enjoyed the service-oriented lifestyle they led, and their generosity touched everyone who knew them. But one trait in their son especially caught my attention.
>
> On our first date, I was pleasantly surprised by the gentleman who walked me to the truck, opened the door, and helped me inside. It was a big, red truck with super-sized tires and I did have a bit of a climb, but he could have just as easily let me face my mountain alone. Instead, he was the epitome of courtesy and his actions made a huge impression on me.

He still opens my doors and waits for me to enter first, even in the rain when I wave him on. Some of my friends marvel at this show of respect, while others reminisce about a time past when they enjoyed such treatment (usually when they were first dating). I just say that I married a Scout and a Scout is courteous!

I appreciate the values Todd's parents instilled in him — values that were reinforced by the Scouting program. Having celebrated over twenty years of marriage (plus the four and a half years we dated), it is nice to know that I can trust that my dear husband will be "polite to everyone regardless of age or position" and that his "good manners [will] make it easier for people to get along together." He is courteous in work and play and models courtesy in front of our children.

As a Scout wife and, now, a Scout mom, I value what the Scout Law has brought to our family. Our family functions on a different level because of this standard; we demand and expect courtesy. While I believe all tenets of the Scout Law are important, I think that each hinges upon courtesy. Gracious consideration of others never goes out of style and is appreciated by everyone.

For the Good of the Cause

Thank you and you're welcome are powerful words. These words are not foreign to a Scout because he is respectful and polite. At home, in school, or in the workplace, a Scout knows that being thoughtful combats rude behavior and that a courteous word shows respect for others. *A Scout is Courteous.*

Kind words can be short and easy to speak,
but their echoes are truly endless.

~ *Mother Teresa of Calcutta*

Life is short. Be swift to love! Make haste to be kind!

~ *Henri Frédéric Amiel*

When I was young, I used to admire intelligent people,
as I grow older, I admire kind people.

~ *Abraham Joshua Heschel*

Constant kindness can accomplish much.
As the sun makes ice melt, kindness causes
misunderstanding, mistrust, and hostility to evaporate.

~ *Albert Schweitzer*

CHAPTER 9

A SCOUT IS KIND

When you face hostile people, you can win them over with kindness. This aspect of the Scout law is much like The Golden Rule, the principle that Jesus taught when he said, "Do unto others as you would have them do unto you" (Matthew 7:12). The Golden rule is not only a Christian principle but also a principle that is found in many religions of the world.

What a Scout Would Do

Kindness can be as simple as sharing a smile with someone you pass on the street or in the store, teaching children how to tie their shoes, or stopping to help someone in need. One Sunday afternoon my wife and I were rushing to church to work with a group of youth. Running behind schedule, I was pushing the speed limit when we passed an elderly couple on the side of the road trying to change their flat tire. With the car jacked high in the air, the gentleman was actually in the trunk wrestling with the spare when we zoomed by.

I made a comment to my wife about this couple in distress, but foot-to-the-floor and the hammer down, I pressed on toward our obligation at the church. However, the sight of that man would not leave my mind. *I'm an Eagle Scout and a Christ follower. Is this right that I pass by someone in need?*

At the next exit, I pulled off the highway to turn around and help that couple. My wife smiled at me and said, "You're going back to help those folks, aren't you?" She continued to smile with a glimmer of approval and a "that's my man" look on her face.

I made my way back and pulled in behind their vehicle. The elderly man was still in the trunk struggling with the spare tire. I introduced myself, and helped him out of the trunk. I pulled the spare out, and safely changed the tire, while my wife chatted with the couple away from the traffic on the busy interstate.

The grateful couple offered me twenty dollars for my services. There was no way in the world that I could take their money. Their appreciation and my clear conscious were all the payment I needed. We drove off and made our way to the church and our appointment with the youth group, and we were only a few minutes late.

Uncle Dave's Trading Post

Once again, we hear from Elizabeth Durham. Her dad, Dave, climbed the ladder of life, not for his own glory, but to place himself in a position to be a blessing to others. His kindnesses are long remembered by the Scouts he worked with — especially those at summer camp.

> As our dad was in charge of the summer trading post at camp, he often noticed that some Scouts were a bit less fortunate than others were. He never made anyone feel less than anyone else, but would often offer "bargains" to these boys and give his words of wisdom as he dispensed their change. The Scouts always left with their purchase, change, a kind word, and felt a bit better after their interaction with "Uncle Dave."

Keeping Watch

Kind words are especially easy to dispense when someone serves you. Being friendly to your waiter or waitress says a lot about who you really are as a person. Bill Swanson, CEO of Raytheon states, "A person who is nice to you but rude to the waiter, or to others, is not a nice person." This may not be the most scientific approach to judging a person's character; however, in my experience, it's a good gauge.

A company who wanted to hire me to work on their leadership team once flew me to a major city to meet with their CEO. It was an enticing offer and I must say that this company really rolled out the red carpet to court me for the position. A member of the team picked me up at the airport and we talked about the possibilities as he drove me to the headquarters.

As we pulled into the parking lot of the organization, the gentleman turned to me and said, "Now, I'm going to walk you through the office, but here is one thing that I need for you to do. No one knows that you are here for an interview and we want to keep this a secret in the office, so if anyone asks, you are an old friend of mine and I'm just showing you around the office." To me, that sounded too much like lying. Red flag number one.

As we walked through the office, my escort introduced me as an old friend and I was quickly taken to the CEO's office. There we found the Chief Officer on the phone, speaking harshly to the person on the other end. Surprisingly, our presence in the room did not discourage his rude behavior. Hanging up the phone, he apologized not for his behavior, but that his wife would interrupt his busy life with (as he put it) "stupid stuff" about the kids. Red flag number two.

My two days with this man led to a third and final red flag. We were having lunch with several of his staff members. As we talked about working together and the importance of teamwork and synergy, I noticed that each time the waitress checked on us, the CEO didn't bother to say thank you, but looked at her with disgust. He finished talking about the team and finally asked, "Well, Todd, when do you want to start work?"

He was shocked when I told him that I would have to pass up the golden opportunity and I thanked him for his time. I started to say that maybe some short-term contract work with me might be productive, but I didn't feel like a full-time slot on their team would be the best for either party.

He glared at me, slid his chair back, and walked out on our meal, as the other team members held their heads down with embarrassment. One quickly spoke up and tried to apologize but

I stopped him because it was not his fault. I returned to my motel room and flew back home thankful that I had not taken the job.

For the Good of the Cause

The CEO I met lived a miserable life. In contrast, I look at men like Dave Durham and many others who modeled kindness in their lives. A Scout knows there is strength in being gentle. Kindness makes him a stronger person than one who bullies his way through life. A Scout treats others as he wants to be treated. *A Scout is Kind.*

Richard Marano (center)
Receiving the Eagle Scout Award

Richard Marano and Troop 39, Waterbury CT (1976)

Todd Shaw (far left, #7)
First Place, Pinewood Derby (1970)

Troop 424 on National TV
1976 American Bicentennial Parade

Troop 424 - Columbia, SC

Virley Seay and Marion Shaw (1975)
Council Camporee

Richard Marano (right)
Presenting Troop 39's Plaque to Camp Mattatuck,
Plymouth, CT (1976)

Richard Marano (far left, seated)
Trading patches at National Jamboree (1977)

Obedience sums up our entire duty.

~ *Hosea Ballou*

I have thought about it a great deal, and the more I think, the more certain I am that obedience is the gateway through which knowledge, yes, and love, too, enter the mind of the child.

~ *Anne Sullivan*

True obedience is true freedom.

~ *Henry Ward Beecher*

Wisdom consists of the anticipation of consequences.

~ *Norman Cousins*

CHAPTER 10

A SCOUT IS OBEDIENT

Obedience can be defined as the act of dutiful or submissive behavior. A Scout pledges to live his life by the Scout Oath and Law, to be obedient to those principles. But why?

From the beginning of time, man has tested boundaries and challenged authority. Even in the history of Rock-n-Roll, popular songs had titles like, "I Fought the Law and the Law Won," which was originally recorded in 1959 by Sonny Curtis and the Crickets, and John Mellencamp's 1983 hit, "I Fight Authority, Authority Always Wins."

So I pose the question again, why should a Scout be obedient to those in authority? Quite simply, it will be a benefit to his relationship to God, his duty to his country, and his own well-being. The Scout Law builds a community and a man at the same time if the Scout is obedient to the principles and ethics of the Boy Scouts of America.

My wife, Lisa, and I have always taught our kids that delayed obedience is still disobedience. All Scout leaders know the drill, you ask a young Scout to perform a task, and you walk off thinking that it is done, only to return and find the job not addressed. You may hear something like, "Well, I was going do it, but..." Chances are that you have experienced this situation many times in your life. You can become frustrated, and do the job yourself — or use it as a teachable moment.

A Strong Foundation for Right Choices

This may come as a shock, but Scouts are not perfect because people are not perfect. The principles of the Boy Scouts of America work if the people work the principles of Scouting. It's just that simple.

I've been in church all of my life, and in Scouting since my days as a Cub. I have a strong foundation and know what is right and what is wrong. However, I have not always lived by those principles that helped shape my life. But, because of my strong foundation, when I was off-track and got tired of messing around in the muck, I knew how to find my way back to the right path of life.

Obedience is the one point of the Scout Law and Oath that is the catalyst for all of the principles in Scouting. You might say that obedience is the glue that holds it all together.

One day my son, Jason, was playing in the backyard with a little friend from down the street. This young man was not in Scouting. Evidently, this boy did not know the importance of obedience. As I worked in the yard, out of sight of the two boys, I overheard this friend ask my son to join him in something that was wrong. I could have jumped in and policed the situation, but I wanted to wait and see how Jason, then a young Cub Scout, was going to respond.

"No, I can't. My Daddy doesn't want me to do that."

"He won't know, come on Jason," the young neighbor said as he tried his best to persuade my son to join him in an act of disobedience.

I'm proud to say that my son stood his ground to the pressures of life.

Age does not grant us immunity from the choice of right or wrong, or from an act of obedience or disobedience. Today as a husband, father, and leader, there is one thing that helps me to stay on the right track and that is to always keep the consequences of my actions in mind.

Vie Herlocker: A Cub Scout and a Hatchet

Stephen Covey said, "While we are free to choose our actions, we are not free to choose the consequences of our actions." When you make a choice, what will be the result of your action? When you answer that one question, you can follow through with a willing heart, knowing that your actions will bring about a favorable result. Scout mom, Vie Herlocker, shares a story of a Cub Scout's choice and its consequences:

> Rule Number One: Do not chop on trees. Justin was nearly eight years old when he received a Cub Scout pocketknife and a hatchet. One day, he headed to his hideout with the new tools, his Scout canteen of water, and a fluff-a-nutter sandwich.

I reminded him of our rule: he could cut honeysuckle vines, but no carving or chopping on trees.

The hideout was under a bramble of wild rose bushes in the pasture behind the house. Several scraggly trunks grew up out of the bramble, and one was rooted in the open space where Justin sat to eat his picnic lunch and to admire his shiny new hatchet. Need I say more?

What harm could a little chip do? One chip led to another, and another, and another. When the trunk toppled over, Justin scrambled out and discovered that he'd felled a sixteen-foot sapling. He ran to the house in tears, apologizing and wanting me to help him fix it. But, unlike gluing the wing back on a broken model plane, the tree could not be fixed.

Justin thought there would be no harm in taking a few whacks, especially since the trunk was hidden from sight. However, hidden disobedience is soon found out. I was proud of him for immediately admitting his wrong and seeking forgiveness. I knew he meant it when he promised to do better next time. Although I forgave him, there still were consequences, including that Justin lost his license to carry the hatchet for quite a while.

Since Scouts try to make the best of every situation, we used the experience to learn more about nature. The sapling had a warty bark and leaves that we did not recognize. So, off to the library we went to discover exactly what he had chopped down. The tree was a Sugarberry tree — a tree not usually found in our area — and very likely the last one to be there!

A Close Encounter

Being a young leader can lead you to trouble sometimes. When I was the troop bugler (something my dad thought that every good troop should have), I found myself in trouble during a campout. On the third day at this particular state park, a tired and weary camper made his way over to where our scout troop was eating lunch. As the camper stood before us, he said, "I would like to know who the bugler is."

I proudly and eagerly spoke up and said, "That would be me, sir!"

He said, "Boy, if you blow that *!@!* bugle in the morning I will—"

Well, I can't say what he said, but having said it, he made his way peacefully back into the woods and my bugle made its way back into my backpack where it remained for the duration of that trip. Because of all I'd learned as a Scout, I felt that being obedient was the best course of action.

For the Good of the Cause

A Scout follows the rules of his family, school, and troop. He obeys the laws of his community and country. A Scout understands that when people break the law, they are only thinking of themselves. Failure to obey the law can bring about death and destruction. If a Scout thinks the rules and laws are unfair, he tries to have them changed in an orderly manner rather than disobeying them. *A Scout is Obedient.*

The cheerful live longest in years, and afterwards in our regards. Cheerfulness is the offshoot of goodness.
~ *unknown*

God loves a cheerful giver.
~ *2 Corinthians 9:7 (NASB)*

A cheerful heart is good medicine.
~ *Proverbs 17:22a (ASV)*

There is one thing one has to have: either a soul that is cheerful by nature, or a soul made cheerful by work, love, art, and knowledge.
~ *Friedrich Nietzsche*

CHAPTER 11

A SCOUT IS CHEERFUL

Scouting taught me to look on the bright side of life and that every problem has a solution. Even though I am more of an introvert, I can still be cheerful. I place my faith in God and trust that He has a divine plan for my life. There is no need for me to walk through life as if I'm attending my own funeral; however, some people do choose to live that way.

Hold the Onions

Several years ago, I owned and operated two sandwich (deli) shops. In the fast food business, or in any type of customer service business, you have to deal with all types of people — and people can be quite rude at times or even downright hateful.

One customer came into my shop on Christmas Eve, right before closing time. We were only open until noon and the main reason that we opened for the day was to make six-foot-long party subs and meat and cheese trays for our customers' Christmas Eve parties. I did most of the special orders that day and I had only one high school worker there to help me and to catch the walk-in orders. When the gentleman came in and ordered his sub, he said "I want everything on it except the onions."

My young worker responded, "That's good because we just ran out of onions." It was true, we used all of our onions on our special orders, and I made the decision not to cut up any more because I did not want them to spoil over the holidays. Now if he really wanted onions, I would have made a special effort to give him onions.

When my employee said that we were out of onions, the man went nuts. He started screaming "What? No onions? What kind of a *!@!* place is this? I want my money back!" He was going crazy and going off on my employee. I was sitting close by at a table drinking a cup of coffee thinking about my own holiday plans when the onion upheaval hit.

"I want to see the manager!" the man exclaimed.

I smiled and asked, "Sir, how may I help you?" He started screaming and cussing at me about the "no onion" situation. I said, "Sir, I don't understand what the big deal is, I heard you clearly say that you did not want onions, so from where I stand there should not be a problem here at all."

Huffing and puffing, he shouted, "I want to speak to the owner right now, give me his *!@!* phone number and I'll call him at home!"

I thought this man was going to have a full-blown heart attack over onions that he didn't want. I smiled and said, "Sir, you're in luck, the owner happens to be in the store now."

The man had this look like, "Now I'm getting somewhere." He should have known that something was up because when I said that, my employee snickered.

I paused, looked at the man, and said, "Hello, my name is Todd Shaw, I'm the owner of this store, and now how may I help you?"

With a look of extreme frustration on his face, he ran out the door shouting profanities. He left his sandwich, he didn't get his money back, and I'm sure he spent the rest of his day in a rage over onions that he didn't want in the first place.

I congratulated my young employee for his high level of professionalism during that heated situation. "Some folks you'll never please, because they look for reasons to be unhappy. Now today is Christmas Eve, so the big thing that we have to do is not to allow that man's bad will to come into our lives and negatively affect the rest of our day."

"Like the cat-kicking story right?"

"Exactly," I said.

He was referring to a story that I told my workers at one of our store meetings. Each week I would share an inspiring story to motivate them to become not only better workers, but also better people. The cat-kicking story is about a person having a bad day, then passing those negative feeling on to others, all because the first person did not deal with the problem. The story goes something like this:

Tom is mad because the morning traffic caused him to be late to work and he is always preaching to his workers that they must be on time. Shortly after getting to work, he yells at Diana, his assistant, about a report he needs. He is not really mad about the report, but he takes his frustration with the traffic out on others and Diana is now the new target.

Diana, the assistant, calls John, the manager who has not turned the report in on time. In a forceful manner, Diana tells the manager to get the report over to her immediately or else. She's not really mad at him, but is passing along the same frustration that she received from Tom.

John, the manager, is upset but complies. After work is over, John is still mad about how things went today at work. His unsuspecting cat walks by the front door just as John walks in. He kicks his cat across the room, and screams, "Get out of my way you stupid cat, what's wrong with you anyway?"

The cat did not do anything wrong, yet John took his frustrations out on the feline. Three people and one poor little kitty had a bad day all because Tom did not properly deal with a setback in his life.

I wonder how many times this story plays out each day on life's highway. A Scout should always look for the good in life and overlook the offensiveness of someone who is obviously having a bad day. A Scout remembers to smile, even under the difficulties of life.

The Bible says, "A person that smiles make other people happy. And good news makes people feel better" (Proverbs 15:30, Easy-to-Read Version). Smiles are truly contagious, and cheerful people can make a huge difference in the lives of others. That is what Scouting is all about, making a difference.

A Cheerful Word

A cheerful word can turn a tense situation around. I have a good friend who lost all of his fingers on his right hand due to a farming accident. People often stare at him and hardly ever hold out their hands to give him a handshake. There are times when people automatically extend their hands, and then when Jo-Jo reaches out, they quickly pull back.

In those moments, Jo-Jo always smiles and delivers a witty comment that puts everyone at ease. One time when a friend's son was biting his fingernails, Jo-Jo looked over at the young man and said, "Hey kid, if you don't stop that, this is what will happen to your fingers. One night in my sleep, I chewed mine all the way down to my fist. Now stop that!"

The kid's eyes grew wide as Jo-Jo shook his fingerless fist in the young man's face. The kid swallowed with a big gulp and said, "Yes sir!" We all laughed at his antics, in fact, we always laugh when we are around him. Jo-Jo is a cheerful person.

Laughter is Good for the Heart

Lord Baden-Powell was on to something when he included *A Scout is Cheerful* in the Scout Law. Being cheerful and sharing a good laugh may improve your health and build stronger friendships.

In a presentation to the Scientific Session of the American College of Cardiology on March 7, 2005, Michael Miller, M.D. reported that laughter may be beneficial to the endothelium — the lining of a person's blood vessels. This lining is where hardening of the arteries begins, and Dr. Miller's team of researchers states that "... given the results of our study, it is conceivable that laughing may be important to maintain a healthy endothelium, and reduce the risk of cardiovascular disease." (www.umm.edu/news/releases/laughter2.htm)

In an article published in *Psychology Today*, "Laughter: The Best Medicine," writer Hara Estoff Marano says, "Laughter establishes — or restores — a positive emotional climate and a sense of connection between two people. In fact, some researchers believe that the major function of laughter is to bring people together. And all the health benefits of laughter may simply result from the social support that laughter stimulates." (www.psychologytoday.com/articles200504/laughter-the-best-medicine)

Every day is Christmas: Dave Durham

One day, I was working around the house with my daughter, and I started whistling the Christmas tune, "Jingle Bells."

My daughter found this a bit unusual, so she asked me, "Daddy, why in the world are you whistling 'Jingle Bells' in July?"

I smiled and asked, "Don't you like Christmas?" She returned the smile and joined me in whistling the tune as we worked.

I love Christmas, but the real reason that I was whistling that holiday tune in July was that I was thinking about Dave Durham. He truly understood that laughter was the best medicine, and could often be heard whistling "Jingle Bells," year round. His cheerfulness was contagious.

For the Good of the Cause

Even while looking at the reality of a bleak situation, a Scout looks for the bright side of whatever he encounters. He understands that a cheerful heart and a good sense of humor not only keep his spirit up, but also build up the morale of others. A Scout keeps a smile on his face even when he is working on the most difficult task. *A Scout is Cheerful.*

**It is thrifty to prepare today
for the wants of tomorrow.**

~ *Aesop*

I believe that thrift is essential to well-ordered living.

~ *John D. Rockefeller*

**Thrift is not an affair of the pocket,
but an affair of character.**

~ *S.W. Straus*

**Waste neither time nor money,
but make the best use of both.
Without industry and frugality, nothing will do,
and with them everything.**

~ *Benjamin Franklin*

CHAPTER 12

A SCOUT IS THRIFTY

A Scout works to pay his own way and to help others. He saves for the future. He protects and conserves natural resources. He carefully uses his time, resources, and property. Being thrifty encompasses all of these things.

Probably one of the greatest products of being thrifty is the fact that you will have a storehouse for a rainy day. Be that money, food, or needed supplies, you are ready for tough times or even better, you are in a position to help those who are in need.

Because a Scout is thrifty, then a Scout can be helpful too. It's amazing how in the Scout Law and Oath, each point is like a rung on a ladder. Each rung takes you higher, to a new level of life, one that will allow you to be an asset to your community, state, nation, and world.

Don Garlits: A Thrifty Man

Someone who truly knows what it means to go fast is Don Garlits, drag racing legend and Eagle Scout. Often we think of successful and famous people as not needing to be thrifty, but Don has a different opinion.

> All of the points of the Scout Law are good and useful, but the one that has served me the best is A Scout is Thrifty, because drag racing did not provide a pension for the participants. I needed to save for my old age and the Scout Law taught me that.
>
> Today, I don't need to rely on government pensions to survive in my retirement. I owe Scouting a lot for this training and I advise all young people to follow in my footsteps, be responsible for yourself, and don't rely on anyone or any entity to provide for you during your old age.

Fast Money

Did you ever pitch pennies when you were young? The players take turns throwing coins at a line or a wall. The player whose coin comes to rest the closest to the target wins all the coins on the playing field.

When I was in middle school, the principal banned the game due to gambling problems and kids losing their lunch money. My Scoutmaster also stopped the game in our troop, and with reluctance, we learned the lesson of A Scout is Thrifty.

Just as we thought that pitching pennies would make us rich without work, Americans desperately want to get rich quick. Television infomercials claim that the key to wealth lies in the purchase of their program. They all promise great wealth with little skills, practically no effort at all, and only minimal time requirements, all while working from the comfort of your home.

State supported lottery systems are among the most advertised ploys to spend a little and win a lot. Why do Americans purchase a record number of lottery tickets in such tough economical times? The promise of winning is a strong and powerful lure for fast money.

Dan Hayes: A Lesson in Gambling

Dan Hayes, Eagle Scout and the Alumni Director of Averett University (Danville, Virginia), shares a story about gambling — at Boy Scout camp — and the lesson the boys learned.

> In 1993, I served as an almost-too-young Scoutmaster for a group of kids going to Camp Powhatan in Virginia. They were playing poker for fake money, bidding millions of dollars.
>
> I wanted them to understand the pain of gambling when you are playing for something of value, so we played for push-ups. When the cards were dealt, I held a dream hand that I knew would win. The kids ran the bidding up to twenty-four and twenty-five push-ups; the lowest bid was eight. I won the hand and wouldn't let them continue playing until they did their push-ups. On the next hand, the Scouts were dropping out of the bidding at two because it was too rich for their blood. In the course of the game, I did do my share of push-ups also.

Way to go Dan! Not a bad way to teach the pain of gambling.

Thrifty with More than Money

In the 1970s, our nation's natural resources were at the forefront of our society's attention, and that focus moved our Scout troop to perform community clean-up projects. One image that still sticks in my mind is the "Keep America Beautiful" campaign and the impact of a particular television commercial with a crying Native American. In the commercial, a car speeds past the Native American (Iron Eyes Cody) and the driver tosses out trash. The camera zooms into Cody's face as a tear slides down his cheek. The announcer then declares, "People start pollution; people can stop it."

The "Keep America Beautiful" campaign combined with the Scout motto, "Be Prepared," made me think about the "tomorrows" of my life. From my money to my health to my land, tomorrows depend on my thriftiness today.

For the Good of the Cause

A Scout keeps his hands busy working for wages and taking care of his natural resources. Saving for a rainy day is not a burden, and makes the Scout prepared for future needs. Taking care of the natural resources allows a Scout to enjoy the wonders of nature and preserve them for future Scouts. A Scout is Thrifty.

Without courage, all virtues lose their meaning.
~ *Winston Churchill*

Courage is going from failure to failure without losing enthusiasm.
~ *Winston Churchill*

Moral excellence comes about as a result of habit. We become just by doing just acts, temperate by doing temperate acts, brave by doing brave acts.
~ *Aristotle*

CHAPTER 13

A SCOUT IS BRAVE

It is difficult to select one point of the Scout Law as the greatest of all twelve points, but I would rank, *A Scout is Brave* near the top. I believe that Teddy Roosevelt would have agreed with me on that. In his speech, "The Man in the Arena," presented at the Sorbonne, Paris, France, on April 23, 1910, Roosevelt describes a brave man as follows:

> It is not the critic who counts, not the man who points out how the strong man stumbles, or where the doer of deeds could have done them better. The credit belongs to the man who is actually in the arena, whose face is marred by dust and sweat and blood, who strives valiantly, who errs and comes short again and again, because there is not effort without error and shortcomings, but who does actually strive to do the deed, who knows the great enthusiasm, the great devotion, who spends himself in a worthy cause, who at the best knows in the end the triumph of high achievement and who at the worst, if he fails, at least he fails while daring greatly, so that his place shall never be with those cold and timid souls who know neither victory nor defeat.

Many of the men who helped shape my life were men who served in our nation's armed services. Whether Army, Air Force, Navy, or Marines, they served with pride and honor, and the way they carried themselves shouted patriotism and bravery.

Brad Bradley: Brave the Dangers of Life

Brad Bradley, a fellow Eagle Scout from Del Rio Texas shares his thoughts on the importance of bravery, not on the battlefield, but in everyday life and business.

> As defined in the Scout Law, "A Scout can face danger even if he is afraid. He has the courage to stand for what he thinks is right even if others laugh at or threaten him."
>
> In my business life, the word brave has taken on several meanings, in combination with other key words related to Scouting:
>
> 1) Be brave enough to take a risk in business, for that is the price of motion. Taking a risk is not inherently dangerous, but it can be unforgiving if a person is not prepared and trustworthy. Always keep yourself mentally awake, for in life and business, you could be tested in a manner that is not morally straight, and without a great reputation, there is no long-term success. Never set aside being reverent in pursuit of life's path, for God puts people in your path for a reason.
>
> 2) Be brave during times of economic storms. You may have to use innovative thinking to make a deal work. Always be cheerful to family, friends, and others during such times and don't make your problems theirs.
>
> 3) Be brave enough, during positive economic times to be thrifty, so that you may be helpful to someone else starting out in business.

4) Be brave enough to seek out and cultivate those who are loyal to improving society.

I've said many times that the Scout Oath and Law are like rungs of a ladder. Brad paints a good word picture of how Scouting allows one to bravely climb the ladder of success.

The Scouting Handshake

As a Scoutmaster, I hold a Scoutmaster's Conference with boys who are seeking a rank advancement. I interview the Scouts just to get a good feel for their understanding and to make sure that they have learned the proper skills to move up to the next rank. I normally start with basic questions and work my way up the Scouting ladder.

One night I had three Scouts to interview. I asked, "Which hand do you use for the Scout handshake?"

The Scout responded, "The right hand."

I looked at him with my eyebrows raised high on my forehead because he had given me the wrong answer.

"Left hand?" he quickly spoke up, but there was uncertainty in his voice this time.

I asked him "Which one is it? Your right, or your left?"

"Right? No, no, no, it's your left hand isn't it?"

"Are you asking me or are you telling me?"

"Sir, I'm not sure," the Scout replied.

After asking all three rank advancement candidates that same question, I was shocked and surprised that none of them answered correctly. I was also upset with myself because I believe that, as a leader, I should take full responsibility for each Scout under my leadership. The boys got the answer wrong because I had not communicated the importance of the Scout handshake.

What is so important about the Scout handshake, and why the left hand and not the right hand? Is this important information for a Scout to know? Should I hold a boy back from rank advancement because he doesn't know the reason? I believe that everything in Scouting is important and has a value.

The Scouts got out their Handbooks, quickly came back to me, and boldly held out their left hand, the correct way to execute the Scouting handshake.

"Are you sure this time?" I asked each one.

"Yes sir!"

"Good, but why do you use your left hand and not your right?"

They did not know, so I shared with them the story about the Scouting handshake.

> According to the Ashanti warrior version of the story, then-Colonel Baden-Powell saluted them with his right hand, but the Ashanti chiefs offered their left hands and said, "In our land only the bravest of the brave shake hands with the left hand, because to do so we must drop our shields and our protection."

The Ashantis knew of Baden-Powell's bravery because they had fought against him and with him, and they were proud to offer the left hand of bravery. (http://www.boyscouttrail.com)

That night at closing, I shared that story with the rest of the troop and closed the meeting by telling them:

You see, as Scouts, you are to be brave. Bravery is not how you feel, but what you do. When others want to walk in the safety of the shadows of the crowd, the brave Scout steps up to the plate and makes a difference in life by standing up for what is right and true. You will have many opportunities in your life to be brave. Let the Scout handshake remind you that you are the bravest of the brave.

Mr. Virley Seay: Bravery in the Battle

Mr. Virley Seay, who started the troop I attended as a Scout, was an incredible man, as evidenced by the memories others have shared about him in this book. Even though he was only around for a short time after I joined the troop, I am pleased to say that I had a few opportunities to camp and learn from him and many more years to hear stories about him. One of my favorites was why he started a Boy Scout troop when he had never been in Scouts as a youth. It all began during the Battle of the Bulge, where Mr. Seay fought as a member of the United States Army.

It seems that in the harsh conditions and the heat of the battle, Mr. Seay and some of his group became separated from their platoon. Without leadership, and unsure of their location, they were hesitant about which way they should go. One of the young soldiers spoke up and said, "If someone has a compass, I will get us back to our unit."

This former Boy Scout led the group safely back to their platoon. Mr. Seay was impressed with the young man's abilities and the training that he had received in Scouting. That day, Mr. Seay made an oath that, when he returned to the states, he would start a Scout troop and train more young men like the one who just saved his life.

I often tell people that I am the product of one man's commitment to Scouting. From the Battle of the Bulge to South Carolina, one man wanted to repay a Scout for saving his life and the lives of others. In the process of repayment, Mr. Seay had an impact on several generations of young men by starting this troop, as well as another troop prior to ours.

Jerry Schleining Jr.: Bravery Calls Your Name

Not all are called to wear the uniform of our nation's armed services. Yet bravery finds its way to the heart of many Scouts. Jerry Schleining Jr. writes:

> The Scout law tells us that a Scout is brave; so, what is bravery and how as Scouts and Scouters should we be brave?
>
> Well, the Scout handbook tells us that, "A Scout can face danger even if he is afraid. He has the courage to stand for what he thinks is right even if others laugh at or threaten him." The handbook goes on to say, "...saving lives is not the only test of bravery. You are brave every time you do what is right in spite of

what others might say. You are brave when you speak the truth and when you admit a mistake and apologize for it. And you show courage when you defend the rights of others."

You don't need a medal to be brave; you don't need ribbons and articles in the paper. Bravery comes from deep inside. The voice within you calls you to do the right thing.

One night at a troop meeting, I was conducting Scoutmaster Conferences. In the course of one of those conferences, a Scout asked my advice about dealing with a certain member of his patrol. Apparently, there had been conflict within the patrol. Nothing so bad that would cause a meltdown, but to the twelve-year-old, the crisis was seemingly insurmountable.

He asked how to deal with this. He was unsure how the other Scout would react and he was worried about tearing up the patrol. I can completely empathize with the Scout and I asked him what he thought being brave meant. He thought it was going into battle or saving a life. While those are demonstrations of bravery, I told him that he was brave for bringing the issue up to me. I also gave him this advice:

If you are right, then stand up for your position. Right wins in the end. When people are in the wrong, they are caught. Those who do things contrary to the Scout Oath and Law are like lightning rods. Lightning rods are designed to attract lightning. Sooner or later, they get struck.

Being brave and standing up for what is right keeps a Scout from being a lightning rod. He is not a target for the lightning strikes of life. As the lightning showers around him, his bravery will see him through the storm.

For the Good of the Cause

A Scout can face danger although he is afraid. He has the courage to stand for what he thinks is right even if others laugh at him or threaten him. A Scout doesn't look for trouble, but springs into action when a need arises. Even though he may be scared, his courage wins out so that he may serve the needs of others. *A Scout is Brave.*

The activist is not the man who says the river is dirty.
The activist is the man who cleans up the river.
~ *Ross Perot*

Let everyone sweep in front of his own door,
and the whole world will be clean.
~ *Johann Wolfgang*

What the country needs is dirtier fingernails and
cleaner minds.
~ *Will Rogers*

My Eagle's upstairs packing; he's cleaning out his
room. He's moving and I should be sad and filled with
lots of gloom.

Oh sure, I'm going to miss him, but I cannot hide my
glee: I have not seen his carpet since 1993.
~ *Vie Herlocker, a Scouting Mom*

CHAPTER 14
A SCOUT IS CLEAN

Sometimes it's hard to get a young boy to stay clean on a camping trip. Most times a troop will come back from a weekend of camping smelling like cowboys off a long hard ride on the trail. During an outing, getting the boys to wash their hands before a meal usually requires a leader standing over them like a prison guard just to ensure that everyone touches a bar of soap. However, there is always that one boy who attracts dirt like a dust mop.

George Hicks: Bart and the Ash Pit

George Hicks shares his Scouting story and about one boy who had a tough time learning that *A Scout is Clean*.

Beautiful fall days are made for camping in the Appalachian Mountains. Normally, Troop 65 of Snellville, Georgia backpacks to all of our campsites, but with new boys just joining the troop we changed our routine for their first camping experience. We planned to drive the Scouts to the campground and take day hikes instead of our normal routine. All of our boys looked forward to camping at Cloudland Canyon State Park, bordering the states of Tennessee and Alabama, and we had a full complement of new and seasoned campers when we left the church.

As soon as we parked the cars and began unloading the tents, one new boy, Bart, ran through the campsite, tripped, and fell into an old fire-pit. As the dust settled, Bart jumped up and began to run, leaving a trail of dust and charred pieces of wood in his wake.

The senior patrol leader stopped Bart, looked at him, and exclaimed, "Look at you. You are filthy. You didn't even bother dusting yourself off. Remember, A Scout is Clean!" (Never mind he ran through camp!)

One of the adult leaders became involved and took the boy aside. Using Bart's cap, the leader dusted off his clothing getting him semi-clean. He reminded Bart about cleanliness, as he briskly flapped the gray dust off Bart's clothing. Using the leader's soap and towel, Bart washed his face and hands at a nearby water pump.

The weekend went by smoothly and all enjoyed the hiking around the rim of the largest canyon east of the Mississippi River. Before each evening meal, the boys lined up in their patrols at the water pump and washed their faces and hands. Afterwards they were encouraged to clean themselves before bed and brush their teeth using the clean theme.

On Sunday morning, we ate a cold breakfast, had a short church service, and packed to leave for our trip home. The boys were moving about the campsite and yes, you guessed correctly, as we called them to their assigned cars, Bart ran through camp and tripped into the old fire-pit once more. Again, he jumped up and ran, leaving a trail of ashes and dust in his wake.

This time the leader who was transporting Bart back to Snellville marched him over to the back of the car to retrieve his gear. Searching for a change of clothing for the dirty Scout, the leader found out that Bart did not bring any gear other than some candy, a tin plate, and spoon for his meals.

So back to the water pump Bart went. As the leader brushed and wiped the dirt from the Scout, he grumbled about a dirty boy riding in his car. All the while, the other boys who wanted to leave began cheering him on by chanting, "A Scout is Clean, A Scout is Clean!"

Making it back to Snellville without further incidence, we waited for the parents to pick up the boys in the church parking lot. Soon Bart's mother, pulling him along, marched up to the gathered leaders.

"Why did you make my son take four baths and the others didn't take a bath?"

The leaders looked at each other with surprise. Bart stood holding his mother's hand. He sported a reasonably clean face, but a pale gray ash covered his ears, hair, and clothes.

The Scoutmaster looked at the boy and asked, "Bart, who made you take a bath?"

Bart sheepishly looked up and said, "You made me wash my face and hands each time I fell into the fire-pit."

The mother looked at her son and said, "Bart that's not a bath, you just washed your face and hands."

"Mom, that's what you call a bath when you're in a hurry," replied Bart.

The mother said not another word, but pulled Bart's dusty body in the direction of her car. The confused boy, not sure of his mother's actions, said, "That's okay mom, remember *A Scout is Clean!*"

I'm glad to say that Bart continued with Scouting, learning not only that *A Scout is Clean*, but also earning the rank of Eagle Scout.

A Clean Body

Many people think that the saying, "Cleanliness is next to godliness," is in the Bible, but it's only a folk saying. Biblical or not, it still holds truth about the importance of cleanliness.

Scouts learn the need for keeping things clean, especially while out camping. The proper storage of supplies will help keep the critters out of your campsite. Raccoons, opossums, and mice carry harmful diseases and can contaminate your food supply. A clean water supply is another necessity, and Scouting teaches boys how to purify water on the trail.

Cleaning your kitchen and cooking utensils is necessary while in the great outdoors, as well. Having the proper wash station and making sure that you keep your hands clean will reduce the spread of germs that can cause diarrhea. An upset stomach while you are camping may be a slight inconvenience to your week or weekend; however, it can become serious if it continues, resulting in dehydration. Cleanliness is a survival skill in the wilderness — whether that wilderness is a drive-in camping area or a backpacking trail far from civilization.

Cleanliness Can Save Lives

I served on a medical mission trip to Haiti with Harvest International. On one trip, we were teaching the Haitians health care. There were doctors and nurses on our team with many years of practical medical training. I was surprised to learn that they were teaching the Haitians the same first aid and camp hygiene procedures that I learned as a Boy Scout.

One of the doctors told me that the number one cause of death in Haiti was not cancer or heart attacks, but that it was diarrhea. I was astonished to learn that with proper training we could offer these people a way to prevent their number one cause of death. I offered my help. The lead doctor on the team asked if I had any medical training. I told him that I was an Eagle Scout; he smiled and said, "You are hired."

The next day, with an interpreter, I taught a small group of Haitians the skills that I learned from my First Aid Merit Badge. Caring for scratches, open wounds, washing hands, and techniques for proper hygiene were covered in our class. One thing that totally astonished me was when one Haitian student asked, "When do you put dung on an open wound?" I laughed at such a statement, but I was the only one laughing. It seems that placing animal dung on a wound was a local folk remedy. We spent the rest of the day covering the proper way to care for a wound and explaining why dung and other home remedies could be harmful.

At the end of the week, we had properly trained twelve Haitian students in first aid. Someone came up with the term and began to call our new students, "Foot Doctors." Others jokingly said, "Oh, you've trained a group of podiatrists." In reality, Haitians walk everywhere they go, so we sent this group of twelve out to help spread the word, and by their feet and training, they would help save the lives of many.

As I watched those twelve Haitians walk off with the first aid kits in hand and armed with this new knowledge, I thought about my Scouting days when I earned my First Aid and Camping merit badges. Those two merit badges helped me to achieve the rank of Eagle Scout, but it was sharing these basic skills that allowed me to help others.

For the Good of the Cause

A clean body, mind, and community — a Scout knows that this will keep him and others healthy and strong. Whether considering personal hygiene, appropriate speech, or suitable relationships, cleanliness points to the Scout Oath where a Scout pledges to keep himself physically strong, mentally awake, and morally straight. *A Scout is Clean.*

The religion of a man is not the creed he professes but his life — what he acts upon, and knows of life, and his duty in it.

~ *Carlyle*

A Scout is reverent toward God. He is faithful in his religious duties. He respects the beliefs of others.

~ *Baden-Powell*

To keep the heart unwrinkled, to be hopeful, kindly, cheerful, reverent, that is to triumph over old age.

~ *Amos Bronson Alcott*

Always and in everything let there be reverence.

~ *Confucius*

CHAPTER 15

A SCOUT IS REVERENT

Faith, reverence, and Scouting go together. Churches and faith-based organizations often charter Scout troops, and many Scouts learn the importance of faith and reverence through Scouting and their local church.

Lord Baden-Powell compared the principles of knighthood to reverence. He described knights as regularly attending religious services, especially before facing battle or difficulty. The knights recognized the importance of their faith not just in church, but they also saw the power of God in the things of creation — plants, animals, and the beauty of the earth.

Baden-Powell said, "No man is much good unless he believes in God and obeys His laws. So every Scout should have religion ... Religion seems like a very simple thing: first, love and serve God; and second, love and serve your neighbors." (1908, p. 231)

Trace Lumpkin: A Time for Faith

Faith is not challenged in the church pew, but in facing the challenges of life. This is especially true with one Scouter, Trace Lumpkin, whose family has remained faithful and reverent through many medical issues and hardships. Here is his story:

My father, brother, and I are all Eagles; my father earned his in 1960 in Cedartown, Georgia. My brother and I were with Troop 151 in Hampton, Virginia. We were active in Scouts and church.

When my dad was about twenty-five years old, he found out he had diabetes. As a kid, I did not know a lot about this disease but as I became older and through Scouts I learned more about it and learned how serious it can be.

As the years went by, the diabetes worsened. At fifty-two, my dad began to have failing kidneys. A couple of years after that he had to take a medical disability and go on dialysis and went on the kidney transplant list. About five years ago, he received a transplant. He now receives treatments every two weeks for fluid buildup in his body.

My brother's daughter, Caroline, was diagnosed with neuroblastoma cancer at the age of two. My brother took her to all the right doctors and now she is cancer free. The cancer was just another bump in the road, but we never lost faith.

Through all the medical issues of the family, our Eagle Scouts have remained reverent. My dad has been brave in all of it. He spends a lot of time in hospitals and doctors' offices. Through all of this, he finds joy in the small things. It was a blessing that he received a kidney when he did. It allowed him the opportunity to have a better quality of life these last five years and for that, I am thankful.

George Jones: The Son of a Preacher Man

George Jones grew up in a home where reverence for God came first. Here is his story of Scouting and faith:

I joined Scouting in 1965 because the organization seemed to have the values that equaled the values we held at home. My father, Walter Jones, was pastor at First Baptist Church in Randleman, North Carolina.

I was looking for other activities to be involved with after school. I needed an outlet with values and structure, and that is when I first heard about Scouting. I asked my mother if I could join the pack or troop. Since, our family was busy with church related activities, I was afraid that we would not have time for Scouting.

Finally, my mother took my youngest brother and me to a troop meeting. At the end of the meeting, the Scoutmaster, I'll never forget his name, Mr. Joe Gagney, walked over and said, "Well boys, are you interested in Scouting?"

I quickly said, "Yes sir, I really am!"

I looked over at my mother and asked her if we could join. She agreed, so we filled out the paperwork right there.

I took my Scouting Handbook and quickly memorized the Scout Oath and Law; I also learned how to tie a square knot, and soon after, I became a Tenderfoot Scout.

Scouting was an environment where the things that I had been learning in the Bible were applied in a practical way. I found that Scouting was that one place where my faith came alive. By doing a good turn each day, the Scout Motto, I was able to put my love for God into practice; I was able to reach out to others in a real and practical way.

My faith has been deeply affected by the Boy Scouts because when you repeat the Scout Oath and Law you make some profound statements: "On my honor I will do my best to do my duty." The idea of honor, best and duty, wow, these were things that were pretty heavy subjects. Basically the Boy Scouts were saying that there was such a thing as honor, there was such a thing as duty, and there was such a thing as doing your best. They didn't say, "On my honor, I will be perfect," but that "I will do my best." The thing that I liked about Scouting was there was room for everybody, whether you were capable of doing things perfectly, or imperfectly, as long as it was your best, there was room for you and a place for you to be recognized.

Even though the Boy Scouts of America is not a religious organization, it embraces character and traditional family values. Despite all the attempts to legally dismantle the organization, it has stood the test of time and has withstood the test of the courts. The Boy Scouts of America was founded upon principles that are both godly and biblical. When you say the Scout Law and repeat those twelve character traits, well I could easily give you ten scripture verses for each one of those.

Faith and Friendship Go Hand-in-Hand

A Cub Scout and a nun walk into a Protestant church... This may sound like an opening to a joke, but this is no joke at all. I was the Cub Scout who took a Catholic nun to his Protestant Church in the 1970s. Attitudes have changed since that time, but in those days, Catholics and Protestants didn't visit each other's place of worship. Sometimes it takes an innocent Cub Scout and a faithful nun to demonstrate the true depth of friendship and to step over man-made barriers.

My mom was an RN and the Operating Room Supervisor at Providence Hospital in Columbia, South Carolina, which was started by and operated under the Sisters of Charity of St. Augustine. Often, while waiting for my mom to finish a shift, I would be entrusted to the care of a very kind Sister Mary Verona. We walked the halls, hand-in-hand, as she carried out her duties or went to Mass.

One day after Mass, I turned and asked Sister Verona, "Sister, I always go to your church. Will you visit mine?" She was touched by my invitation and later that day we talked over the plans with my mom. After receiving approval from Mother Superior, a date was set.

When the special day arrived, we drove across town to pick up our guest of honor. What a sight we must have been walking up the steps of that crowded church! I'm positive the members were a bit perplexed to see me, a Protestant Cub Scout, escorting a Catholic nun attired in her traditional habit.

Although her visit might have made some uncomfortable, including the pastor who admitted later that preaching in front of Sister Verona was his most challenging to date, she remained peaceful and secure. Her demeanor exuded faith and her gentle squeezing of my hand showed her understanding of the awkwardness of the situation. Her warm smile of assurance communicated to me that what we were doing was right and was the beginning of breaking down those barriers of intolerance held by some.

My association and friendship with this dedicated nun taught me that faith is more than a once a week sermon, but a daily choice to extend mercy and grace to others. Scouting reinforced that lesson by teaching tolerance and respect for others' faith while holding onto my own faith with confidence. Today, I strive to help others look beyond differences, and to treat all with dignity and honor, no matter what their religious beliefs. When others might have seen a Protestant Cub Scout and a nun, I just saw two friends going to worship together. Isn't that what being reverent is all about?

For the Good of the Cause

Being reverent is more than going to a place of worship once a week. A Scout is strong in his faith and worship, and respects the practices of others. Being reverent is revealed in the way a Scout acts and treats others. *A Scout is Reverent.*

Scouts winning a 4H Competition (1965)
(left-right: Brad Bradley, Ronnie Adams,
Bo Hutto, Bud West)

Brad Bradley (left)
Receiving the Rank of Eagle Scout (1964)

George Hicks - Philmont (July, 1959)

George Hicks (July, 1959)

Trent and Trace Lumpkin
Eagle Scout Court of Honor (1986)

Trace and Trent Lumpkin
Eagle Scout Court of Honor (1986)

Trent and Trace Lumpkin working on their
Eagle Scout project

Three Generations of Shaw Scouts
Todd, M.B., and Jason Shaw working at
The Federation of the Blind Annual BBQ Dinner

How can we know ourselves? Never by reflection, but only through action.
Begin at once to do your duty and immediately you will know what is inside you.

~ *Johann Wolfgang Von Goethe*

Do the duty which lies nearest to you, the second duty will then become clearer.

~ *Thomas Carlyle*

Never give in, never give in, never, never, never, — never — in nothing, great or small, large or petty — never give in except to convictions of honor and good sense.

~ *Winston Churchill*

CHAPTER 16

DUTY

As any Scout can tell you, there are three parts to the Scout Oath: duty to God and country, duty to others, and duty to self. A Scout measures achievements against this high standard and the pressures of his peers do not sway him. A Scout pledges to live his life by this standard and to be an influential leader.

Do Your Best

Growing up, my family members often told me, "When a task has once begun, you leave it not until it's done; and be a matter great or small you do it well or not at all!" (And my wife always adds, "... and 'not at all' is *not* an option for my kids.")

When I worked on my grandfather's tobacco farm, he expected my best in every task that he assigned me. If it was feeding the hogs or chickens, or servicing the tractor, I could always count on one thing: he was going to drop by and check on me to see if I needed any help, had any questions, or to see if I was through. Then he would inspect my work.

I have taught this same principle to my kids, and I sum it up like this: I expect your best, then once you have finished, I want to see if you have done your best.

One day I assigned my kids the task of picking up the sticks in their grandparents' front yard. After about an hour of working, I stepped outside to see how they were progressing. I overheard my little girl giving my son, who is now a Boy Scout, this admonition: "Jason, you better do a good job! You know Daddy's going to come out here to inspect our work. You better give it your best!"

In Scouting, you learn to do your best because a Scout knows that actions speak louder than words. Your actions back up your promise, and your promise is your word.

A Life of Service

In my book *Out of the Box and Loving It*, I talk about duty to God and a life of service. I'd like to share this passage from that book:

> The Bible speaks of you as a "laborer" and says that you should use your gifts, abilities, and time wisely to glorify God and serve others. Because, "...we are God's masterpiece, He has created us anew in Christ Jesus, so that we can do the good things He planned for us long ago" (Ephesians 2:10 NLT). Notice that He planned "good things" for you long ago. Therefore, you should wake up each day, with a zeal and passion, trying to discover what good things that God has in store for you today. That is your daily mission in life.
>
> And work to "Do your best to present yourself to God as one approved, a workman who does not need to be ashamed and

who correctly handles the word of truth" (2 Timothy 2:15). "Being confident of this, that he who began a good work in you will carry it on to completion until the day of Christ Jesus" (Philippians 1:6).

"God has given each of us the ability to do certain things well. So if God has given you the ability to prophesy, speak out when you have faith that God is speaking through you. If your gift is that of serving others, serve them well. If you are a teacher, do a good job of teaching. If your gift is to encourage others, do it! If you have money, share it generously. If God has given you leadership ability, take the responsibility seriously. And if you have a gift for showing kindness to others, do it gladly" (Romans 12:6-8, NLT).

It all comes down to you, and how you serve! Those good things prepared by God are put there, and have been there for a long time just waiting for you to unearth them. You have to make up your mind that you are going to get your hands a little dirty and get on board with what God has planned for you. So are you with me? (Shaw, pp. 20-21)

Patriotism

Several years ago, I took my kids to the Veterans' Day parade in Columbia, South Carolina. The Army, Air Force, Navy, and Marines all have bases in South Carolina and their presence makes this parade a spectacular sight.

I looked forward to the opportunity to teach my kids about patriotism and the meaning behind this special day. We arrived one hour early to get choice seats by the review stand, where the military top brass gather to observe the troops as they march by in rank and file. Naturally, all the service members stand a little taller as they pass by their leaders.

It didn't take long for the bleachers around us to fill up with veterans — all wearing their hats indicating the branch and war they served in. An older couple, who had served in the Korean War, caught my attention. They arrived a few minutes after us and placed their lawn chairs at curb side.

Soon the Master of Ceremonies stepped up to the microphone and called everyone to attention as the color guard presented the colors of our nation. Thousands of spectators stood and recited the words of the Pledge of Allegiance; it was a moving experience and one that made me proud to be an American.

A military band played a rousing John Phillips Sousa march. You could feel the patriotism in the air — and that was what I wanted my kids to experience. People cheered, flags waved, and grown men wiped away their tears as our nation's colors passed by for review.

I noticed the veterans sitting in front of us and to our right. Still nursing wounds from battles fought on foreign soils, they feebly stood to their feet each time our nation's flag passed by. The pride and joy on their faces as they viewed the troops marching down the city street was inspiring.

However, one person was about to change the dynamics of the section that we were sitting in. A young woman, probably in her early twenties, pushed her way through the crowd. She had a cell phone at her ear and a baby on her hip. With no demonstration of regard for those who had arrived before her or respect for the purpose of the parade, she positioned herself directly in front of the elderly Korean War veterans, and continued speaking loudly into the phone.

The female veteran politely tapped the young woman on the back and said, "Excuse me please, you are blocking our view." The young woman did not move, but turned up her nose and continued her cell phone conversation. Three times the elderly veteran made her plea; finally, the young woman took the phone from her ear and announced, "I'm going to stand right here and there ain't a *!@!* thing you're gonna do about it!"

I jumped out of the bleachers to call for a nearby police officer. As he made his way over to investigate the situation, the young woman pushed her way through the crowd in retreat.

A bystander shouted, "You didn't have any right to do that! You didn't have any right to call the police on her!"

I was amazed that someone old enough to know better would stand up for such poor behavior. I responded, "Ms., you're joking right? You're telling me that what that young woman did was okay in your book?" At that, the police officer interrupted me and asked that I move on and not cause any more problems.

Oh boy, now I was the troublemaker. Frustrated at the rude woman, frustrated by the bystander who accused me of wrong, and now frustrated with the police officer, I turned to my kids and commanded, "Move out, we're going home!" With two small kids in tow, I moved down the sidewalk like a man on a mission.

Then my little girl said, "Daddy, can I watch one more band?"

I want to tell you, there is not a dad alive who could deny a request like that. Therefore, I smiled and said, "Sure honey, we can watch one more band."

As I stood there, I tried not to let that negative experience ruin my day. I focused my attention on the enthusiastic crowd, and smiled myself as I watched my kids sway to the music. Then a young Marine caught my attention.

He looked to be in his early twenties and was wearing his dress blues. His arm was in a sling, he was wearing a patch over one eye, and he was missing part of one ear. It appeared that these were battle wounds, perhaps from the Iraqi War.

But he was not alone. His parents and his young wife were all decked out in their Marine attire. I could tell that it was a proud moment for this family. The father then stepped out in front to take a group photo.

Todd, why don't you be helpful and get over this funk you're in? With that thought, I stepped forward and asked, "Sir, may I take that picture for you, so you can stand next to your son?"

"Yes, please. That is kind of you, sir!"

"Move in tight and give me a big smile. Ready? Everyone say *cheese!* Alright, that is a great picture."

As I gave the camera back to the dad, I noticed a tear running down his face, he tried to thank me again, but he was overcome by his emotions. Soon the entire family was crying, maybe they were touched by the moment or just thankful to have their son and husband back home.

I turned to the young Marine. "I am proud of you son. I want to thank you for serving our country. Semper Fi!"

As I looked in the young man's scarred face, his body full of battle wounds, I could see that he was still a boy in many ways. He too fought back the tears, maybe appreciative that someone said thank-you, or maybe proud that he had the opportunity to serve his country. He stood up straight, shook my hand firmly, and gave me a hardy "Ooh Rah!" (That is what a Marine shouts when he is fired up!)

By that point, the Marine was crying, his wife was crying, the parents were crying, and I was crying too. My kids looked at me like, "We can't take Dad anywhere. In one day, he's had a run-in with the law and he's made a Marine cry. What next?"

I guess I have thought about that day a million times. I think about that rude, rebellious woman and I think about that proud Marine. I have tried to analyze the difference between them. They were both about the same age, but had two different spirits about them. One had a selfish attitude of take, take, take; the other had a selfless heart of service, commitment, and honor. One sought to satisfy her own desires. The other sought to serve his country, no matter what sacrifice would be required of him. What made one willing to give and the other wanting to take? I believe it all comes down to choice and influence.

I don't know if the young Marine was ever in Scouting, but one thing is for sure: from an early age, someone impressed upon his life the ideas and values that are the core of Scouting.

Like the men and women who proudly serve our country in the armed services, when I was a Boy Scout, I learned this same pride and respect for our country. We began each meeting by saying the Pledge of Allegiance to the flag. We learned the proper way to handle, fold, and even retire the flag from service.

During America's bicentennial celebration, my Troop 424, from West Columbia, South Carolina, marched in over twenty-five parades with flags that marked each step of our country's independence. That year we were ambassadors for our nation and we even appeared on national television when we marched down the streets of Atlanta, Georgia, during the 1976 Fourth of July celebration.

Because of this service to our country, the Freedom Foundation at Valley Forge presented our troop with a special bicentennial award for outstanding achievement in bringing about a better understanding of the American way of life.

As a Scout makes his way to the rank of Eagle, there are fifteen required merit badges. Each one focuses on a specific part of the Scout Law and/or the Scout Oath. Three of the required badges relate solely to citizenship (Citizenship in the Community, Citizenship in the Nation, and Citizenship in the World). By earning these three merit badges, following the religious guidelines, understanding the workings of economics, and fulfilling the requirement for community service projects, every Scout has a strong understanding of what it truly means to be an American.

Purchasing Tomorrows

The saying, *"You purchase your tomorrows today,"* can apply to so many different areas of our lives but probably applies best when it comes to our health. If children and adolescents are obese, they are at risk for health problems during their youth and adulthood.

I never was a super athlete as a youth, and it was not until my sophomore year in high school that I began to play soccer, my first attempt at organized sports. Yet, I was in good physical shape because of my involvement in Scouting. We played games, hiked, rode bikes, canoed, and many other physical activities.

Each year, our troop participated in and received the Presidential Physical Fitness Award. Why? Because the Scout oath includes remaining physically fit. Perhaps Baden-Powell agreed with Winston Churchill's belief that healthy citizens are the greatest asset any country can have.

After high school I wanted to remain true to the Scout Oath by remaining healthy, so I enrolled in Karate classes. In less than four years, I reached the rank of Yudansha (1st Degree Black Belt). I competed in the Karate tournament at the Palmetto State Games and took fourth place in the forms (kata) and third place in the heavyweight fighting (kumite) divisions. The next year I took first place in two out of the three Black Belt divisions. Those were proud moments and I really enjoyed training.

The camaraderie in our dojo (karate school) was strong and we pushed each other to become more physically fit. We made our workouts a competition in an effort to bring out the best in each teammate. One challenge was to do as many push-ups as you could in thirty seconds. I held the record by doing forty-three.

I was feeling good about my accomplishments and even more confident in my push-up record. That all ended when a Major in the Marine Corp changed my thinking. One evening we were competing for the "push-up king," and once again, I came through with my forty-three push-ups to retain my title.

I was laughing and enjoying my victory probably a bit too much, and Mr. Doug Perry, a Marine, shouted out, "Who has the record?"

"I do, sir; it's forty-three in thirty!" I probably said it with a little pride in my voice. You see, I was in my mid-twenties and Mr. Perry was fifty-five years old. I had been whipping up on young bucks for some time; I was the push-up king! I thought, *"Now some old Marine thinks he's going to come along and dethrone me? Yeah, right."* Say it with me: *pride comes before the fall.*

Mr. Perry looked around the room, making sure that he had everyone's attention and shouted, "Time me!" He hit the deck and that old man started pumping out push-ups like a machine. The clock was ticking and he showed no sign of slowing.

When the clock keeper called time, Mr. Perry jumped to his feet. "What's my count?"

To everyone's amazement, the counter said "Fifty-five push-ups in thirty seconds!"

My reign was over, I was dethroned, and there was a new king in town. I stood there speechless as Mr. Perry walked over to where I stood and pressed his finger into my chest. "One push-up for every year that I am old and don't you ever forget that either."

"Sir, yes Sir!" The man certainly had my respect and that feat of physical superiority only inspired me.

I learned a valuable lesson that day, on many levels, but one that has stuck with me (second only to *pride comes before the fall*) is that physical fitness is not just for the young. Mr. Perry beat my record because Marines know that physical fitness is an indispensable aspect of leadership.

More than twenty years later, the impact of Mr. Perry's lesson is still with me. I no longer train in the Martial Arts, but I am still fit. I watch what I eat and how much I eat, and because of that discipline, I don't battle with my weight. I don't go to the gym, but I still do push-ups and sit-ups in my basement.

As Mr. Perry showed me, I want to show my Scouts the importance of physical fitness. When I am working with the Scouts who are earning the rank of Tenderfoot, I do the required push-ups, pull-ups, sit-ups, long jump, and quarter-mile run with them.

Why do I stay in shape? I am a Scout and I owe it to myself to stay fit. By example, I can teach a younger Scout that we purchase our tomorrows today. Physical fitness is a lifetime investment.

For the Good of the Cause

The nature of man is tridimensional: mental, physical, and spiritual. When you have a tridimensional oath and a tridimensional man, nothing is overlooked when it comes to building up the health, character, and faith of a Scout. However, words without actions to back them, are only words.

It's better to look ahead and prepare than to look back and regret.
~ *Jackie Joyner Kersee*

If you are prepared, you will be confident,
and will do the job.
~ *Tom Landry*

The best preparation for tomorrow is doing your best today.
~ *H. Jackson Brown Jr.*

I will prepare and some day my chance will come.
~ *Abraham Lincoln*

CHAPTER 17

FORWARD THINKING

The Scout Motto, *Be Prepared*, contains only two simple words, yet they are words that will solve many of life's problems. In good economical times, you need to prepare and save for a rainy day. When tough times come, the prepared person will have what he needs. Being prepared also applies to being ready for unexpected open doors.

Being prepared is more than a motto; it is the only way to live life. Have you ever thought about why your car comes with a spare tire? You never know when you will have a flat tire, but you can drive with confidence when you know you are prepared.

When I lived in Florida, the weather was always changing, and as any Floridian will tell you, "If you don't like the weather, just wait five minutes and it will change." Residents of the Sunshine State respect the hurricane season and know the importance of being prepared. They don't wait until the winds and rain are raging to buy water, board up their windows, or make an evacuation plan.

But, what does it mean to really be prepared? Being prepared is more than having a generator for hurricane season or a spare tire in your trunk. Being prepared is a thought process. My friend, Dr. Jay Strack, calls it "future-tense thinking."

Jim Dalton: Be Prepared and Be Persistent

Abraham Lincoln said, "If I had eight hours to chop down a tree, I'd spend six hours sharpening my ax." This is not only a good principle if a Scout is working to earn his Paul Bunyan award or his Totin'Chip, but it also applies to being prepared for whatever obstacles and opportunities come in life. Professional Scouter, Jim Dalton, shares how preparation and persistence opened doors of opportunity for him in life:

> Scouting has been a tremendous influence on my life. I began my adventure in the "Wonderful World of Scouting" in 1952, at age twelve. I was in Troop 85, sponsored by the Galax (Virginia) Lodge of the Loyal Order of the Moose. I had a great experience in Scouting and advanced to Eagle Scout, an award that is my most cherished recognition. I fondly remember my Scoutmaster, Cobb Adams, the local postmaster. He was a wonderful leader and role model. Most of all, he put the "outing" in Scouting.
>
> I attribute the experiences of my youth in Scouting for developing the foundation of my life. A young boy does not join Scouting to develop good character or to become a good citizen. However, the patrol method, the emphasis on teamwork, and the strong principles of the Scout Oath and Law instill these values over time. Quality volunteer leadership and well-planned outdoor adventures provide the foundation for Scouting.

I graduated from Galax High School in 1959 and then attended Hiwassee Junior College in Madisonville, Tennessee. I returned to Galax during the summer of 1960 as lifeguard at the Galax Country Club swimming pool. In 1961, I met with Graham Brest, the District Executive of the Carroll-Grayson District of the Blue Ridge Council of the Boy Scouts of America, to discuss employment as Waterfront Director at Camp Powhatan, the Boy Scout summer camp for our area. My uniforms and meals were a complimentary benefit of the position. The salary of seventy-five dollars per week was good too, considering I would be able to save almost all the salary from camp for college expenses.

I attended Schiff Scout Reservation and completed my certification as Waterfront Director. I successfully completed courses in swimming, life saving, rowing, canoeing, and waterfront administration. My most difficult experience at National Camping School was rowing. I struggled with keeping my oars in the open "Davis Row-locks." The commands of "catch, pull, feather, recover," were repetitious and meaningful; however, I was not able to coordinate my body movements with the commands. I labored all week with this challenge and only succeeded due to a caring instructor who worked with me each day at "twilight time," an optional free-evening volunteer instruction time.

My rowing instructor was the kind of person who did not give up on me. On the morning prior to the certification ceremony, he was down at the waterfront at 6:30 a.m. working with me with a never-give-up attitude. In order to receive my certificate I had to pass all the skills. Without certification in rowing, I would not receive my certificate in waterfront administration. At approximately 9:00 a.m. that Saturday morning in 1961, everything came together — the catch, pull, feather, recover became coordinated with my upper-body and with back straight and body totally coordinated, I moved the boat in a straight line at his commands. I made excellent port and starboard pivots and made a command port landing at the dock. I was amazed that it seemed so easy. The instructor was so excited for me and the bottom line is that I received my certification that day and it was one of the best events of my life.

When I returned to Camp Powhatan for the staff training week, I really felt prepared. I wanted to be like my rowing instructor and help other young Scouts.

During Staff Week at camp, I continued to work during free time to perfect my rowing skills. I became highly proficient in rowing and decided that I would be the lead instructor in Rowing Merit Badge at camp. I would also be the lead instructor in non-swimmer instruction. I made the decision that it was a greater and more rewarding challenge to teach a person how to swim rather than to teach a Scout how to swim better.

I had a successful and rewarding year as Waterfront Director at Powhatan. The next year in 1962, the Blue Ridge Mountains Council was planning to open a new camp developed totally on the patrol method and they asked me to be the first Aquatic Director at Camp Ottari. I was proud and challenged by this opportunity and we had a great year and achieved an A rating by National Camping Standards the first year of operation. This experience showed me the true meaning of the Patrol Method and the significant part that teamwork plays in the development of the patrol and the quality reinforcement of the troop.

This was not the end of the story, just a wonderful early beginning for me. After graduation from the University of Knoxville in 1963, I entered the education profession as teacher and coach at Oliver Springs Junior High in Anderson County, Tennessee. At the end of one year of teaching, I was attracted back to the wonderful memories of my Scouting days and especially memories of the Scouting professionals that I met while serving as Waterfront Director in summer camp. This led me to inquire more about professional Scouting.

I entered the Scouting profession on May 24, 1964, as District Executive of the Cherokee District of the Great Smoky Mountain Council, Knoxville, Tennessee.

During my forty-one-year career with the Boy Scouts of America, I had the opportunity to extend my expertise in the aquatic area. The opportunity of professional service with BSA has provided many wonderful experiences and most of all the reward of working with the best volunteers in the movement. Obviously, I have made many Scouting friends. Another award that I remember most prominently was when a group of Scouters who volunteered additional time to build a chapel at Camp Barstow in Columbia, South Carolina, awarded me a simple, hand-made plaque at a closing campfire making me an "honorary volunteer." One of my favorite people, Scoutmaster Berg Simpson, presented it to me.

It is hard to put everything in perspective and there is a tendency to ramble when you have walked as many miles on the Scouting trail as I have. I will now attempt to make the closing point of my story, "Be Prepared and Be Persistent." As previously stated, my aquatic background provided many opportunities of greater service to the BSA. I was privileged to serve on the Aquatic Staff of seven National Camp schools at Boxwell Scout Reservation in Middle Tennessee Council and served on the Aquatic Staff at National Jamborees and the 1967 World Jamboree in Idaho.

The close to my story is related to National Camping School at Boxwell. It was there that I was primary instructor for Rowing and Life-saving for training potential Waterfront Directors for BSA summer camps across the region. When you consider the difficulty I had with rowing, you see that persistence and being prepared paid off. It was there in the mid-1960s that I had the privilege of association with Greg Tucker, a candidate for

Aquatic School Certification from the Middle Tennessee Council in Nashville. Greg was highly proficient in all aquatic areas and completed his certification in Waterfront Administration. Greg had many significant achievements along the Scouting trail and later became a prominent attorney and financial advisor in the Washington, D.C. area. He later retired to his farm in Readyville, Tennessee, and currently serves in positions of leadership on the Southern Region and National BSA committees. He has also served as President of Area 5 of the Southern Region.

Greg is one of the most knowledgeable authorities in the BSA on Scouting Aquatics. He has directed numerous National Aquatic Camping Schools, served as advisor to the National Council on Aquatic, Health, and Safety issues, and contributed most prominently in the development of the aquatic-related merit badge pamphlets and instructional literature for National Camping School.

One of the most memorable events in my life happened prior to my retirement when Greg presented me with the most recent edition of the Rowing Merit Badge Pamphlet, which he had signed, recognizing me as his mentor and rowing instructor. This is noted even more significantly in the closing page of the pamphlet where he publicly makes this acknowledgement in print. This brought back the memories of my rowing instructor at Schiff Scout Reservation. I truly believe that the days of my youth in Troop 85, guided by Mr. Adams, helped me to "Be Prepared and Be Persistent."

For the Good of the Cause

One of my favorite race car drivers, Mario Andretti, said, "Circumstances may cause interruptions and delays, but never lose sight of your goal. Prepare yourself in every way you can by increasing your knowledge and adding to your experience so that you can make the most of opportunity when it occurs." A Boy Scout is prepared for life's obstacles and opportunities.

We cannot live for ourselves alone. Our lives are connected by a thousand invisible threads, and along these sympathetic fibers, our actions run as causes and return to us as results.

~ *Herman Melville*

Those who bring sunshine into the lives of others cannot keep it from themselves.

~ *James M. Barrie*

A tree is known by its fruit, a man by his deeds. A good deed is never lost; he who sows courtesy reaps friendship, and he who plants kindness gathers love.

~ *Saint Basil*

CHAPTER 18

GOOD TURNS

In 1918, the American Red Cross Magazine commissioned Norman Rockwell to paint a picture to accompany their story commending the Boy Scouts for their home front efforts during World War I. Rockwell painted a young Scout assisting an older man across the street on a blustery winter day. The painting is known by two names, "The Daily Good Turn," and "Scout Helping Gentleman Across Street." This same illustration became the cover of the February 1919 issue of Boys' Life. (www.best-norman-rockwell-art.com)

And So the Story Goes

I read a funny story about a Scoutmaster who challenged his Scouts to live out the Boy Scout Slogan, *Do a Good Turn Daily*. The young Scouts eagerly left the meeting that night ready to fulfill their commission.

One week later, all the boys reported their kind deeds and selfless acts of service. The Scoutmaster clapped and praised the young men for their honorable acts. However, one boy hid himself in the back of the room hoping not to be seen by the leaders.

The Scoutmaster noticed the lone Scout. "Johnny, do you have a story to share?"

The Scout lifted his head and the Scoutmaster saw that the young man had a black eye. Surprised that this young Scout would get himself into a fight, the leader asked, "So, how did you get that black eye?"

"By doing my good turn," he replied with his head hung low. The troop all chuckled at his response.

The Scoutmaster quickly spoke up and called the troop to order, and asked Johnny what happened.

"Well, I was coming home from school and I saw a little old lady with a bag of groceries standing on a street corner. I told her I'd help her, and then I took the bag from her, grabbed her hand, and helped her across the street."

"Well, that sounds like a wonderful good deed, but that doesn't explain why you have a black eye."

The Scouts waited to hear Johnny's explanation. After a dramatic pause, he said, "She didn't want to cross the street."

Don Capps: Appreciation for Sighted Guides

It seems that being a Scout and being helpful are the same. When I was a youth, my troop worked (and still works) with Mr. Don Capps of the Columbia Federation of the Blind on their annual BBQ fund-raiser. Mr. Capps happens to be blind himself. The Scouts worked as sighted-guides as the federation clients went door-to-door selling tickets. During that time, I assisted a man by the name of Marshall Tucker. Mr. Tucker was a piano tuner by trade and a great man who loved a conversation. Later in life, he was honored when a country rock band from Spartanburg, South Carolina, named their band after him, "The Marshall Tucker Band." Those times matured young boys into men, taught us many valuable lessons, and brought interesting people into our lives that we may not have met otherwise.

I recently reconnected with Don Capps, who is now the President Emeritus of the National Federation of the Blind of South Carolina, and reminisced with him about how the Boy Scouts served that organization. Here is what Mr. Capps said:

> Having worked closely with your father, M.B. Shaw Jr., and his Boy Scouts for several decades, no doubt I have a wealth of information to share as the decades go by and soon we forget many of these important life experiences.

> Without the assistance of your father, who dedicated his life of service to the Boy Scouts and young people, I would never have had the tremendous benefit of being served by the Scouts.

> Since the late 1960s, I have had the great fortune of working with many Boy Scouts. In the three-night canvas just prior to our barbecue, the blind call upon the Federation Center's neighbors. I am proud to state that not one time did my much-appreciated Boy Scout guide cause me to sustain any accident, as the Scouts were so careful and hard working.

> Having worked in the private sector for forty years, and learning

much about Columbia's business community, I have realized that Boy Scouts contribute mightily with their time, energy, and commitment in the annual three-night canvas.

Unquestionably, the Boy Scouts I worked with beginning in 1968 have gone on to choosing their lifetime partners, having their own children, and working in many different career fields. While the years have gone by, frequently I recall these many Federation initiatives resulting from Boy Scouts serving as sighted guides. Long ago, I realized the tremendous good the Boy Scouts do in our community. I deeply value their labor of love, as these wonderful boys are always so kind and helpful.

The Boy Scout project with the blind is exceptional. Boy Scouts and their leaders played a huge role in the success of this barbecue. Boy Scout programs not only exist to bring out the best in the boy, but they afford the Scoutmaster the opportunity to develop each Scout's maximum potential with some becoming Eagle Scouts. One Columbia area Scout became an Eagle Scout by painting the Federation Center as a project. Many of our nation's leaders became Eagle Scouts, which is the foundation for the greatest possible service to our country.

For the Good of the Cause

In 1928, James E. West, the first Scouting executive in America, wrote:

While Scouts should not be expected to "parade" their services, it would be helpful if Scout Leaders, parents, and others would encourage boys in the doing of Good Turns, and recognize the difference between normal household and other chores, and actual Good Turns. Selfishness is almost a universal evil. Certainly, it is overcome by the Scout Program, which is based upon the development of service for others, and the Daily Good Turn is an important factor in the development of a habit of service and attitude of mind, which offset a tendency to selfishness. (www. inquiry.net/ideals/deeds/)

How far you go in life depends on your being tender with the young, compassionate with the aged, sympathetic with the striving, and tolerant of the weak and strong. Because some day in life you will have been all of these.

~ *George Washington Carver*

The critical responsibility for the generation you're in is to help provide the shoulders, the direction, and the support for those generations who come behind.

~ *Gloria Dean Randle Scott*

The future belongs to those who believe in the beauty of their dreams.

~ *Eleanor Roosevelt*

CHAPTER 19
WORDS TO LIVE BY

When parents unfamiliar with Scouting inquire about signing their sons up, they often ask about the age-range. My usual response is, "Eleven-years-old to eighteen-years-old for Eagle, then..."

I deliberately don't finish the sentence. After my unusual pause, the parents will ask, "Then what?"

"Then, how long a Scout stays involved after his eighteenth birthday is up to him. I've been Scouting for forty years. My dad is in his eighties and still involved. Scouting never really ends, or at least it shouldn't."

Scouting is an organization that generates a lifelong following. It is common to hear Scouters say, "Once a Scout, always a Scout," or "Once an Eagle, always an Eagle."

Boy Scouts proudly celebrate their heritage on the eighth day of February, which is the birthday of Scouting in America. "Scout Sunday" is the first Sunday in February, a day when places of worship recognize the young people and adults for their contributions through the BSA. On Scout Sunday, I proudly wear

my uniform to worship and when the pastor asks for all Scouts —
current and former — to stand, I eagerly search the room for those
who have also been impacted by the Boy Scouts of America.

Scouting never ends. A Scout's days of being a card-carrying
member may end with his youth, but Scouting is a lifelong quest
for truth and knowledge, and a journey of duty, honor, and service.
The Scout Law and Oath continue to be words to live by.

Jerry Schleining Jr.: Always Learning

Jerry Schleining Jr. is a Scoutmaster in Oregon and the host of the
Scoutmaster Minute Podcast and Blog. As a Scout, Jerry was in
Troop 100, in Brunssum, Holland (Transatlantic Council, BSA), and
Troop 249, in Ft. Polk, Louisiana. Jerry writes about a Scoutmaster
conference with a young Scout — and the lessons both Jerry and
the Scout took away from spending that time together:

> I have the pleasure of sitting down with the Scouts in my troop
> and having Scoutmaster Conferences. One in particular was with
> a young man finishing his Tenderfoot badge. We went through
> the standard questions and he passed with flying colors.
>
> Then we got to talking (my favorite part of the conference).
> This is where you really learn about the boy and what makes
> him tick. It also is a great way for the Scout to feel comfortable
> chatting with adults. I asked this young man which of the twelve
> points of the Scout Law he could do better at. Typically, you get,
> "obedient," "cheerful," or "My Mom says I need to be clean and
> work on my room," but this little guy said "kind."
>
> I asked why he thought that. He went on to say that he had

some anger issues and that he needed to be kinder. Further, he talked about the stress and pressures of his life.

So I asked myself, what kind of pressures and stress could an eleven-year-old possibly have? He described some, and we won't go into that here, but let's just say they were not all that bad, but the discussion opened up a guided discovery for both him and me.

What we learned was that if he took just twelve little words and applied them to his daily life, all of his stress would go away.

He stressed about having to do chores, so I told him that instead of making them out to be something horrible, to be cheerful and smile while he did the dishes, or whatever his task. We went example after example about how the Scout law could make his life better.

I talked to him about what I call the twelve-point check, just like when you get your oil changed. Check twelve points and you will be good to go.

I explained that if he could answer yes to each of the twelve points, then he would never have anything to stress and worry about.

Are you being Trustworthy?

Are you being Loyal?

Are you being Helpful?

Are you being Friendly?

Are you being Courteous?

Are you being Kind?

Are you being Obedient?

Are you being Cheerful?

Are you being Thrifty?

Are you being Brave?

Are you being Clean (in body and mind)?

And, are you being Reverent?

Answering yes means that you are doing the right thing, a no answer means you need to work on it. These are only twelve little words, but they can teach you a lot about yourself. Others see these twelve little words in you.

Now, I'm not sure how an eleven-year-old boy is stressed out; life sure will be tough if he doesn't get that under control. I hope that a twelve-point check will help him. It sure helps me.

I am always learning. Every day of my life I learn something. What I learned at that Scoutmaster conference was that this great little kid will grow up to be a good man. He wants to live the Scout Law and with that in his pocket, he will do great things.

He may not be the next president or rocket scientist, but he will be a man who can be counted on, because he has the Scout Law.

I learned more about that young man in fifteen minutes than his friends will ever know. I am grateful for that time. Never shut the door to learning; it's not always in a classroom that you get an education. And, you will be amazed at how much an eleven-year-old will teach you.

Bill G. Griffin: I've Earned Mine

One evening, I quizzed a group of young Scouts on the meaning of each point of the Scout Law. When I got to *A Scout is Thrifty*, not one boy could really tell me what it meant. I gave them my explanation but I could tell that my words never really made a connection with them. As young Scouts grow with experiences, and mature into adulthood, the words of Scouting will find meaning and purpose in their lives. Bill Griffin shares how a few words can have a big impact when you truly understand their importance.

> My dad, William (Bill) C. Griffin, understood the importance of propagating the Boy Scout program into the future. He recognized this most of all in the small circle of troops he helped lead and the boys he had contact with. His understanding of this importance can't be focused on any single principle of the Scout Law, but more on the Scout Law in its entirety.

> "I've earned mine, now go and earn yours!" These words burned me to my inner soul. I didn't know why, but I knew they were important. My father was an incredible teacher, but I did not realize that for many years. While my sister and I were going through the possessions of a fifty-plus year marriage, just after the loss of our mother, we found some documents we'd never seen before. (Dad had predeceased our mother by seven months and we needed to settle the affairs.) We found newspaper clippings, certificates, and a magazine article from a trade journal highlighting Dad's role as Eagle Scout Board of Review Chairman. This article caught my eye and I studied it closely.

> Dad never attained the rank of Eagle Scout, although he had

been a Scout as a boy. I remember him telling me that he almost made First Class but their troop had become inactive due to World War II. He never forgot the ideals of the Scout Law and Oath and lived them throughout his career in the Air Force, civilian trades, and most of all, as a Scout Leader in the 1960s and 1970s.

As an airman in the United States Air Force, he rapidly attained rank. He was an intelligent man, but lacked the college education necessary for an officer's commission. This did little to hold him back as a leader. His career spanned the early development of the Air Force, the Korean Conflict, the introduction of jet aircraft, and President Kennedy's challenge of the moon landings and the Cold War. His involvement in each of these monumental milestones of the U. S. Air Force remained as some of his proudest legacies right up to the time of his death, which was fittingly on Veterans' Day 2002. He retired from the Air Force in August 1969 as Chief Master Sergeant William Constantine Griffin at a ceremony that also awarded him the Air Force Commendation Medal for his contributions to the manned space programs and the defense of our country through the strategic missile programs.

For several years prior to his retirement, he enjoyed his role as Assistant Scoutmaster to my troop in Cheyenne, Wyoming. We camped, canoed, and explored the Rocky Mountains of Colorado and Wyoming as well as the plains of Central Wyoming and Nebraska. We fished the mountain streams and "enjoyed" many cold winter adventures. He relished his role as a Scout Leader and took extra pains to make sure that as Scouts, we knew not only the skills for advancement, but also the purpose of each in the everyday world.

It was in this mountain paradise that I attained the rank of Eagle Scout. I use the word attained because I feel that I would never have made it without the encouragement, and sometimes forceful, efforts of my dad. My Eagle leadership project would have never been accomplished without the "requirement" that we work on it every Saturday morning until it was completed. Through his encouragement and wisdom, on May 23, 1969, in front of the Chief Justice of the Wyoming Supreme Court, I passed my Eagle Board of Review and became the third Eagle Scout of Troop 118, Cheyenne, Wyoming.

My Eagle Court of Honor went off without a hitch. I stood proudly before the troop and received several other awards and merit badges and then the time came for me to receive my Eagle recognition.

Chief Justice John J. McEntire presented the Eagle Charge. My mom pinned the medal on my uniform and I pinned a small Eagle pin on her dress. Then my dad placed the Eagle neckerchief around my neck and cinched it up tight. As he did so, he said those infamous words, "I've earned mine, now go and earn yours!"

It would be nearly thirty-two years before I understood what he meant. After ten years as a Scout leader myself, my son finally had passed his Eagle Board of Review and a Court of Honor was being held in his honor. His mother proudly pinned his Eagle Medal to his uniform and it was my turn to place the Eagle Neckerchief around his neck. Memories flooded back and as I cinched it up tight around his neck, I uttered the words of my father, "I've earned mine, now go and earn yours!" As I did, I looked around to my own dad who was in the audience smiling. I had finally earned mine.

It's Your Turn

Ninety percent of the time, I was enthusiastic about the Boy Scouts and I loved being involved in my troop. I eagerly awaited

Scouts each Thursday evening, and since I lived just up the street from our Scout hut, I was normally the first one there. However, I can recall one night that I had a terrible attitude about Scouts.

That night, my dad noticed I was not standing by the door chomping at the bit to walk down the street. He asked if I was going to Scouts, and I responded by rolling my eyes for dramatic effect, and mumbled something like, "I don't know. Maybe I will, or maybe I won't." I'm sure I played the part of a typical teen with an attitude that night.

My dad just looked at me and said, "Todd, we have Scouts tonight and I'm going. It's my responsibility to be there, and besides, I happen to enjoy Scouts." With that matter of fact statement, he walked out of my room. I was thinking about his words when I heard the front door shut.

I turned to my window and watched my father make his way to the Scout hut.

I ran to my closet, put on my beloved uniform, and bolted down the street to join my friends and my dad. I flung open the door to the Scout hut and found my troop performing the opening ceremony for the night. I jumped into the rank, threw up my hand, and joined in saying the Scout Oath and Law.

Tom Landry, the former coach of the Dallas Cowboys, said, "Leadership is getting someone to do what they don't want to do, to achieve what they want to achieve." When my dad walked out that door in his uniform, his action influenced my decision to go to Scouts. Whether he knew it or not, he motivated me to do what

I didn't want to do; he provoked me to get off my butt and get over my pity party. I was inspired to go to the meeting — to follow through with what I truly wanted to achieve.

The Bible also speaks of being an inspiration: "Think of ways to encourage one another to outbursts of love and good deeds" (Hebrews 10:24). The Greek word used in this verse for *encourage* is *par-ox-oos-mos* which literally means *to incite, stimulate or irritate.* Did you catch that last word? Leaders can be a little irritating at times and that is perfectly fine as long as they have a spirit of love and goodwill.

However, true leadership comes down to this one point: lead by example. Say all you want to say, teach all you want to teach, but if your actions do not back up your words, then you are wasting your breath.

Baden-Powell knew that leadership was by example when he stated, "Show me a poorly uniformed troop, and I'll show you a poorly uniformed leader." On another occasion, he said, "Success in training the boy depends largely on the Scoutmaster's own personal example."

That night, when my dad walked out the door, he helped create discipline in me, and that is something that is lacking in many today. Yet discipline is something that the Boy Scouts of America can instill in young men, if the leadership inspires through personal example.

For the Good of the Cause

Chief Scout of the World Baden-Powell (Scoutmaster Handbook, p. 9) said:

> But the real way to get happiness is by giving happiness to other people. Try and leave this world a little better than you found it and when your turn comes to die, you can die happy in feeling that at any rate you have not wasted your time but have done your best. Be prepared in this way to live happy and die happy — stick to your Scout Promise always — even after you have ceased to be a boy and God help you do it.

The Scout Oath and Law do not cease to exist in a young man's life just because he has aged-out as a Scout. Years of knowledge and truth have been poured into his life, and discipline is the bucket that draws from the well of a Scout's experiences. He is prepared for life and plans for every day, but is flexible enough to handle the unexpected.

A man asked me, "Were you an Eagle Scout?"

"No sir, I never was, but I still am. Once an Eagle, always an Eagle."

Scouting has done so much to prepare me for my life. Now it's my turn to say to the next generation, "We have Scouts tonight and I'm going. It's my responsibility to be there, and besides, I happen to enjoy Scouts."

After all, *A Scout Is...*

REFERENCES

Baden-Powell, Robert. 1908. *Scouting for Boys*, Les Longeray Boreal, France: World Scout Brotherhood Edition of Scouting for Boys.

"BSA Adult Membership Annual Report." 2008. http://www.scouting. org/About/AnnualReports/11memsummary.aspx

Califano, Joseph A. Jr. 1999. "Accompanying Statement to the National Survey of American Attitudes on Substance Abuse V: Teens and Their Parents." August. The National Center on Addiction and Substance Abuse at Columbia University.

Carrison, Dan and Walsh, Rod. 1999, 2005. *Semper Fi, Business Leadership the Marine Corps Way*. New York, New York: AMACON

Chapel Hill Academy, "Student Essay." www.chapelhillacademy.net/ docs/ Thanksgiving% 2520 Essays.doc+Boy+scouts+has+made+a+differen ce +in+my+life&hl=en&ct=clnk&cd=2&gl=us

Dobson, James. http://www2.focusonthefamily.com/docstudy/ newsletters /A000000331.cfm#footnote14l.

Marano, Hara Estroff. 2005. "Laughter: The Best Medicine." www. psychologytoday.com/ .../ 200504/laughter-the-best-medicine -

Miers, Don. Excerpt from Williams, Pat.2008. *Coaching Your Kids to be Leaders: The Keys to Unlocking their Potential*. FaithWords.

Roosevelt, Theodore. 1910. "The Man in the Arena." Speech presented at the Sorbonne Paris, France, April 23. www.theodore-roosevelt.com/ trsorbonnespeech.html

Rowe, Mike: Online Chat, posted March 7, 2006. http://dsc.discovery. com/fansites/dirtyjobs/chat/transcripts/06march07/06march07-08.html (accessed June 16, 2009)

"Scouting Handshake Origin Minute." http://www.boyscouttrail.com/
content/minute/ scout_handshake_origin-252.asp

"University of Maryland School of Medicine Study Shows Laughter Helps
Blood Vessels Function Better." 2005. www.umm.edu/news/releases/
laughter2.htm

West, James E. Scouting Quote. www.inquiry.net/ideals/deeds/

Wiersbe, Warren. 1990. *Be Satisfied*. Colorado Springs, Colorado: David C.
Cook.

Popular Quotations used throughout this book were collected from
these websites:

www.bartleby.com

www.brainyquote.com

www.heartquotes.net

www.thinkexist.com

Contributors' Biographies

Eddie Albert

Eddie attended Scouts through middle school in the Indian Waters Council, in South Carolina.

He met his wife, Sharon, in the Airport High School band in 1980. In October 2009, they celebrated their twenty-fifth wedding anniversary. Eddie and Sharon are now very involved with the band at White Knoll High School where their youngest daughter, Jordan, is a junior and captain of the Color Guard. Their oldest daughter, Kristen, is a sophomore at Converse College where she is majoring in music.

Eddie majored in commercial art and graphic design at the University of South Carolina. He pursued a career in art that quickly collided with computers. After purchasing a Macintosh in 1987 to do freelance art, Eddie realized that the future of graphics was going to be computer based and he left his job to sell computers to designers, ad agencies, and in-house graphics departments. For the next several years, he strengthened his skills and contacts as he worked with printers and graphics departments throughout North Carolina, South Carolina, and Georgia. Eddie is currently the pre-press manager at RR Donnelley in Columbia, South Carolina where he has worked since 1994.

Brad Bradley

Brad earned the rank of Eagle Scout in 1964, in Del Rio, Texas. He recently accepted a position as a Director with the Concho Valley Boy Scout Council, based in San Angelo, Texas. He has been married to his wife, Jo Marie (Stark) for forty-three years. They have two sons, one grandson, and a granddaughter.

Brad continues to run the swine marketing business he bought in 1971. Working with contract swine farms across the nation, Brad's business produces specialized pork that is marketed to domestic natural food stores and to the export market.

His community service includes: past president of the Hill Country Livestock Raisers Association; past president Llano Athletic Boosters; past board member of the Llano Memorial Hospital; past director with the Llano Chamber of Commerce; pre and post NAFTA Advisor to U.S. Department of Agriculture, National Pork Producers Council, and USDA Agriculture Marketing Service; and past Wagon Boss with the West Texas Boys Ranch. Brad served with the National Pork Producers Council Steering Committee, Task Force and Interim Board of Pork America, Inc. and American Pork of Iowa, LLC. He has served with the San Angelo Stock Show and Rodeo Association for more than thirty years, and helped establish a Del Rio Wildcat Alumni association and Website. (www.delrioalumni.org/joomla)

Contributors' Biographies

Paul Bragg, II

Paul joined Scouts as a Cub and earned his Eagle Scout rank with a Silver Palm in Troop 53, in Jackson, Ohio. His wife and two children are also involved in Scouting in various capacities.

Paul is currently Scoutmaster of Troop 57 in Wellston, Ohio. In addition, he is an Advisor of Crew 110 in Jackson, Ohio; Chief Logan District Camping Chair; Simon Kenton Council Camping Committee; and Simon Kenton Council Venturing Committee.

Paul grew up in Jackson, Ohio, and graduated from Jackson High School in 1990. Following that, he attended Ohio University and was a member of the Marching 110. During Desert Shield/Desert Storm, Paul joined the United States Marine Corps with the help of Senator John Glenn. He was discharged after being injured during training, and returned to school.

Paul graduated from Ohio University with an Associate in Applied Sciences (Law Enforcement Technology) in 1992, and a Bachelor of Criminal Justice in 1998. He also attended Shawnee State University in Portsmouth, Ohio and earned his Paramedic certification in 1997. He further received his Ohio Peace Officers Certification from Ohio University-Chillicothe in 2001.

Paul was a member of the Jackson Fire Dept for thirteen years as a firefighter, Hazardous Materials Technician, Confined Space Rescue Technician, and Certified Fire Safety Inspector. He is a member of the Jackson County Sheriffs' Auxiliary and is presently employed by Southeast Ohio EMS as a Paramedic.

Donald Capps

Although Don was never a Scout, he has had an ongoing relationship with the Scouting program since the late 1960s, supporting many troops by providing opportunities for service hours and Eagle Scout projects. He and his wife, Betty, have two children, Craig and Beth, and two grandchildren.

The youngest of eleven children, Don grew up on a tobacco farm in rural South Carolina. Due to congenital glaucoma, he was born without vision in his left eye and seriously impaired vision in his right eye. In 1947, Colonial Life and Accident Insurance hired him as a junior claims examiner trainee. As his eyesight deteriorated, however, he felt resigning was his only option. However, the company president did not agree and noted that Don's value to the organization was due to many other abilities besides reading. He went on to enjoy a thirty-eight year career with the company before retiring in 1985.

While successful in business, Don's greatest achievements were in his countless hours as a volunteer. Because of his lobbying efforts, more than thirty-five legislative acts designed to improve the lives of blind people have passed the South Carolina Legislature. His work resulted in the creation of the South Carolina Commission for the Blind, a state agency that provides orientation and adjustment to blindness, rehabilitation, and job-placement services.

Don was recently named President Emeritus for the National Federation of the Blind and was awarded the "Order of the Palmetto" by the Governor of South Carolina. The Palmetto award is one of the highest honors a citizen can receive for service to the state. Although Don has retired from business, he remains active with the Federation.

Contributors' Biographies

Jim Dalton

Jim joined the Boy Scouts of America in 1952 as a twelve-year-old. He went on to earn the rank of Eagle in Troop 85, sponsored by the Galax, Virginia Lodge of the Loyal Order of the Moose.

Jim devoted his forty-one year career to Scouting. As a professional Scouter, he held the following positions: District Executive, Cherokee District, Great Smoky Mountain Council 1964-1969; District Executive M/P (Multiple Person), Pellissippi District, Oak Ridge, Tennessee, 1970-1973; Field Director, Great Smoky Mountain Council, 1973-1974; Director Field Service, Great Smoky Mountain Council, 1975-1976; Scout Executive, West Tennessee Council, 1976-1981; Scout Executive, Indian Waters Council, Columbia, South Carolina, 1982-1990; Area Director, Southeast Region, BSA, 1990-1995; Personnel Director, Southeast-Southern Region, BSA, National Council BSA, 1995-2005.

Today, Jim is retired and enjoys spending time with his family and fishing.

Bill Dial

Bill earned the rank of Eagle Scout. He grew up in West Columbia, South Carolina, and was actively involved in Troop 424 as a boy. As an adult, he was an Assistant Scoutmaster, and is an active supporter and contributor to Friends of Scouting in Anderson, South Carolina.

Bill graduated from the University of South Carolina with a bachelor's degree in Business Administration. He is the Chief Financial Officer for The Apex Automotive Group of South Carolina — a group of five new vehicle franchised dealerships in Anderson and Myrtle Beach, South Carolina.

Bill currently lives in Anderson and has been married to his wife, Rynde, since 1990. They have two children, Drake and Kathleen. Drake is a Star Scout with Troop 215. Bill's family is a member of Holy Trinity Lutheran Church in Anderson. In his spare time, Bill enjoys the outdoors with his family, and hunting, and offshore fishing.

Contributors' Biographies

In Memory: Davis M. Durham

(November 2, 1923–November 29, 1997)

Although never a Scout as a boy because his parents had no means of transportation, Dave became involved in Scouting in the 1950s while he was running his grocery store. He was still a bachelor and volunteered as a leader for the troop at Emmanuel Lutheran Church. When his business began to interfere with his Scouting, he pursued professional Scouting as the District Scout Executive for the Indian Waters Council in Columbia, South Carolina. He was a member of the Order of the Arrow, Vigil Honor Classes 1964. His Indian name was "Shot in the Leg."

After retirement, Dave continued to serve the Scouting community by running the Trading Post at Camp Barstow until his passing.

In 1991, the governor awarded Dave with "The Order of the Palmetto." This award is the highest civilian honor in the state of South Carolina, and recognizes a person's lifetime achievements and contributions to the state.

Dave was married to Gladys (Branham) and had two daughters, Madeline and Elizabeth.

Donald Glenn Garlits

Don earned his Eagle Scout rank in Troop 49, Tampa, Florida. He is married to his high school sweetheart Patricia (Bieger). They have two children, Gay Lyn and Donna, and five grandchildren.

Don, "Big Daddy," Garlits is considered the father of drag racing. He was a pioneer in the sport and perfected the design of the rear-engine "top fuel" dragster. His Swamp Rat series of 34 hand-fabricated race cars carried him to 144 national event wins, 17 world championships, and numerous other racing milestones. Because of his innovative designs and record-breaking accomplishments, Swamp Rat XXX is enshrined in the Smithsonian Museum of American History and in 2002, Swamp Rat XXXIV ran 323.04 MPH at the Gator Nationals. He further contributed to the sport when he opened the Don Garlits Museum of Drag Racing in Ocala, Florida, in 1984.

Contributors' Biographies

Billy Gray Griffin

Billy earned the Eagle Scout rank in 1969. He and his wife, Connie, have three children, Melinda (husband Jimmy), Phillip, and Jeffrey (Eagle 2001), and two grandchildren, Taylor and Wyatt.

Billy currently serves as the Assistant District Commissioner for the Etowah Creek District and is the Eagle Scout Board of Review Chairman for Etowah Creek. While in Wyoming, he was inducted into the Order of the Arrow and became a Brotherhood member in 1968. He served as a Chapter officer for several years and was on the original Chy-Kola Chapter dance team. He has received the NESA Scoutmaster Award of Merit, the District Award of Merit, and The Lamb Award, an adult religious award.

In 2006, he took the role of Indian Waters Shooting Sports Coordinator and was certified at BSA National Camp School in May of 2006. On March 13, 2008, he was awarded the Silver Beaver, the highest award a Boy Scout Council can bestow on a volunteer Scouter. He held many various positions such as Assistant Cub Master, then "crossed over" into Troop 870 with his son as Scoutmaster, Committee member, and Advancement Chair.

He has been employed by SCANA Corporation since 1979 and currently is the supervisor of the Geographic Information Department in Columbia, South Carolina. He serves his community as a thirty-three year volunteer with the Lexington County Fire Service as a Captain with the Amicks Ferry Fire Department. He received the 2007 Firefighter of the Year from the South Carolina American Legion.

Dan Hayes

Dan earned the Eagle Scout rank in Troop 212, Chelmsford, Massachusetts. He is currently serving as a Cub Scout Den Leader.

He grew up in Scouting and progressed into working at Boy Scout camp. He had the opportunity to work at four different council camps. He credits Scouting with making him who he is today.

Dan was born and raised in Massachusetts, but has lived in Virginia since 1987. He is employed as Alumni Director for Averett University, in Danville.

Contributors' Biographies

George W. Hicks

George earned the rank of Eagle Scout with one palm, in Troop 189, Baltimore Area Council, Baltimore, Maryland. He began his career in Scouting in Georgia as a Scout leader and held a variety of troop positions.

After he and his wife, Maggie, retired, they moved back to his ancestral home near Winston-Salem. Because he wanted to keep his string of consecutive years of Scout leadership current, he immediately located a troop sponsored by Palmyra United Methodist Church.

George currently serves within the Northeast Georgia Council and Old Hickory Council (North Carolina) as the Public Relations Chairman within the Hanging Rock District, Stokes County, North Carolina, and Troop 408 Committee Chairman.

George was fortunate as a boy to have a father committed to Boy Scouts and dedicated adult leaders who were WWII veterans. After the war, men from his church started the community's first Boy Scout troop. These men provided a sense of value and heritage within his economically modest community.

Scouting guided him to activities with like-minded boys who enjoyed the outdoors. Scouting's values, integrity, and leadership training helped George in life as he went to college, raised a family, and worked in the telecommunications industry.

Dr. George Jones

George earned the rank of Eagle with six palms in Troop 518, in Grays Chapel, North Carolina. He is a Vigil member of the Order of the Arrow and served our country in the United States Air Force.

Today he serves as the reservation chaplain for the Blue Ridge Mountains Council at Camps Powhatan and Ottari and works with Life Outreach Ministry in Lynchburg, Virginia. www.lifeoutreach.com.

George and his wife, Ann, have been married for 34 years and both of their sons are also Eagle Scouts.

Contributors' Biographies

Roderick Kohl

Roderick earned the Eagle Scout rank with three palms in Troop 267, in Oklahoma. He is currently serving the BSA as an Assistant Scoutmaster with Troop 267.

As a college student attending University of Science and Arts of Oklahoma, Roderick is working toward a bachelor in art degree with a theatrical concentration. He began scouting as a Bear Cub and has remained active ever since. Roderick feels that his time in Scouting is worthwhile, and that the time he invests in working with younger Scouts is not only an investment in their future, but also an investment in his own.

Bob Kornegay

Bob earned the First Class Scout rank before his parents moved to Harkers Island, North Carolina where there was no Scouting program near by. Even though his Scouting as a youth may have been brief, Bob saw the importance of the BSA. He currently serves within the Blue Ridge Mountains Council in the Catawba District as a Unit Commissioner and a Committee Member for Troop 2, also in the Catawba District. He has gone to Philmont seven times.

With a degree in music education from East Carolina University, Bob taught high school band for a number of years; then he opened a music store in the Roanoke area. Once Bob was asked to fill-in as a Choir Director for a local church until they found a replacement. Bob stepped up to the plate — and it took the church twenty years to find a replacement.

Bob has lived in Virginia since 1965 where he loves to hunt and fish. His son is an Eagle Scout.

Contributors' Biographies

Trace Lumpkin

Trace earned the Eagle Scout rank in Troop 151, in Hampton, Virginia. He currently serves as Assistant Scoutmaster with Troop 284, Galax, Virginia and is a member of the Order of the Arrow.

Scouting runs deep in his family. He is the son of Eagle Scout, Harry Lumpkin; brother to Eagle Scout, Trent Lumpkin; proud husband of Girl Scout leader, Sherry Lumpkin; father to Second Class Scout, Austin Trace Lumpkin; and Girl Scout, Savanna Lumpkin. He does his best to put the oath and law to work every day in his job at the Galax Recreation Center as the Aquatic Coordinator. Trace is also the swim coach of the Galax Riptide and teaches swim lessons using many of the skills he learned while attending summer camp.

Richard M. Marano, Sr.

Rich earned the Eagle Scout rank with a Bronze Palm in 1977. St. Francis Xavier Church, Waterbury, Connecticut, sponsored his Troop 39. He grew up in Waterbury, and now resides with his family in Oxford. He and his wife, Eileen, have three children: Michelle, Rich Jr. (an Eagle Scout with Silver Palm), and Christine. Rich enjoys boating and water sports.

He is currently president of Housatonic Council, Connecticut; Assistant Scoutmaster of Troop 1, Oxford, Connecticut; and Chairman of Religious Emblems for the Archdiocese of Hartford Catholic Committee on Scouting.

As a Boy Scout, Rich was an active member of the Mattatuck Chapter of Eluwak Lodge #59, and served as Tap-Out Chief. He was also a Youth Member of the Archdiocese of Hartford Catholic Committee on Scouting, and attended the 1977 National Scout Jamboree.

Rich has been a Connecticut Superior Court judge since 2004. He has served as president of the Waterbury Bar Association, the Connecticut Criminal Defense Lawyers Association, the Connecticut Young Democrats, and the Connecticut Italian American Bar Association. In 2003, he was voted "Waterbury's Best Lawyer." Rich has been honored as an honorary Mayor of Waterbury, and received the Good Citizen Award from the Connecticut Sons of Italy. The Vice Consul of Italy also honored him for promoting his Italian heritage. He is a recipient of the Humanitarian Service Award from the Boys Club of Waterbury.

Rich is the author of four books: Growing Up Italian and American in Waterbury; Connecticut Criminal Legal Forms (Volumes I and II); and Vote Your Conscience: The Last Campaign of George McGovern. www.richardmarano.com

Contributors' Biographies

John C. Matthews

John earned the rank of Life Scout in Troop 343, West Columbia, South Carolina. He and his wife, Susan, met while members of Explorer Unit 424. They have two daughters and have been blessed with three grand kids.

John served his country in the Navy. After returning home from Vietnam in 1970, he agreed to serve as Cub Master. His sister, Patricia Privette, agreed to be the Den Mom. John spent many afternoons and weekends carving out pinewood derby cars. He last served as Cub Master (1972-1980), Pack 424, West Columbia, South Carolina.

John has been a member of The American Legion Post 90 in West Columbia, South Carolina for forty-one contiguous years. He served as commander for a total of twenty-two years. He joined the US Postal Service in 1990 as a building Equipment Mechanic and served as an Acting Supervisor when needed.

Bill McCutcheon

Bill enjoyed eight years in Scouting and earned the rank of Eagle in Troop 899, Conway, South Carolina.

Bill attended University of South Carolina 1968-1970 and Campbell College 1970-1972. Today he is the President and CEO of the American Kart Racing Association. He has over thirty years of karting experience as a shop owner. He served as a World Karting Association Trustee and National Director and developed many local, state, and national karting programs. (www.akrainc.com)

He served Covenant Baptist Church as Director of Music from 1985-1992. Bill enjoys spending time with his wife at their mountain home.

Contributors' Biographies

Jim Moore

Jim earned the Life Scout rank in Black Mountain/Swannanoa, North Carolina.

Scouting began for Jim in 1957 where he joined a cub pack in Montreat, North Carolina. Franklin Graham was in his pack, so Jim was exposed early to the Graham family — little knowing he would one day work for him.

In 1960, Jim's family moved to Swannanoa where he joined a great Scout troop. He stayed in Scouting, working as senior patrol leader for a new troop formed at his church in Black Mountain, and served with a new Explorer Post in Swannanoa until his high school graduation.

After a tour in Vietnam with the USMC and eight years working for United Merchants in Old Fort, Jim found his career as a biomedical technician at St. Joseph's Hospital in Asheville. In 1998, he was offered a position with Franklin Graham's Samaritan's Purse in Boone, North Carolina, where he is currently doing international medical relief.

Jim has been married to Mary (Walker) Moore of Black Mountain for 41 wonderful years.

Jerry Schleining Jr.

Jerry earned the Life Scout rank. He began his Scouting life as a Cub Scout in Virginia and he became a Boy Scout in Holland after he earned his Arrow of Light. As the son of a soldier, Jerry lived all over the world. He had the unique experience of being a Scout in the Transatlantic Council, where many of his fondest memories were made.

Currently Jerry is serving as a Scoutmaster in Troop 664 in Gresham, Oregon. He is also a Scoutmaster for the Cascade Pacific Council's National Jamboree contingent for 2010. Jerry is the host for the highly rated Scouting Podcast, "The Scoutmaster Minute," where he shares tips and ideas about the Scouting program. (www.thescoutmasterminute.net)

Contributors' Biographies

David Smoot

David earned the rank of Eagle Scout in Troop 231, Decatur, Georgia. He married Patricia Diane Wiggins in 1972. They have two daughters: Jennifer Smoot Miles, Cleveland, Tennessee; and Erin Smoot Jones of Jacksonville, Florida. Jennifer has two girls of her own: Chandler Brooke, born in 2003, and Riley Madison, born in 2007. Erin is expecting her first child in December 2009. It's a girl, Emma Renee!

David was ordained into the ministry in 1975 and served seventeen years as an associate pastor in Decatur, Georgia before going full-time in missions in 1992. He has served as Missions Pastor of Wings of Faith Fellowship in Ocala, Florida since 1995.

David's foreign missions travels have taken him to Barbados, Cuba, Jamaica, St. Vincent, Trinidad, and Tobago in the Caribbean; as well as ministry in Brazil, England, Ghana, Hungary, India, Mexico, Nicaragua, Nigeria, Romania and Wales.

Roland (Roe) Young

Roe earned the rank of Star Scout in Troop 424, West Columbia, South Carolina. His greatest joy is his wonderful daughter, Cayman.

He received a Bachelor of Science degree in Business Management from Winthrop College and has been a State Farm agent for twenty-one years. He supports various charities, is a past-president of the Lions Club, a member of the Business Association of Columbia, and is a board member of the South Carolina Council on Economic Education.

INDEX TO SCOUTERS, CAMPS, COUNCILS, TROOPS, AND CONTRIBUTORS

ABOUT THE AUTHOR

In 2010, Todd Shaw will celebrate his fortieth year as a Boy Scout. He received his Eagle rank in 1980, and he continues to work with the Boy Scouts of America as an Assistant Scoutmaster of Troop 284, in Galax, Virginia, and as a District Chaplain for the Mountain Empire District of the Blue Ridge Mountains Council. Todd is a member of the Order of the Arrow, a life member of the NESA, and is currently earning his Wood Badge tickets.

Todd is an author, professional speaker, and the founder and president of On Track Ministry (a motorsports outreach ministry). The principles he teaches are based on scripture, and the Scout Law, Oath, and Motto. Todd is a master storyteller, and his heartbeat is application. His enthusiasm, quick wit, and humor engage the reader or audience and motivate them to action.

In the work place, Todd's background includes construction, healthcare, owning and managing several restaurants, owning an automotive shop, and serving as a youth pastor. He holds a 2nd degree black belt, and taught karate for several years.

Todd and his wife, Lisa, live on the Blue Ridge Parkway in Galax, Virginia. They have a son, Jason (a Second Class Scout aiming for Eagle!) and a daughter, Krista. When not writing, speaking, or working with Scouts, Todd enjoys racing, watching re-runs of the Andy Griffith Show, drinking coffee, telling stories, and riding his motorcycle.

If you would like to learn more about Todd, or to contact him concerning your next Scouting, non-profit group, military, church, or corporate event, visit:

www.ontrackTodd.com

www.ontrackministry.com / Motorsports outreach ministry

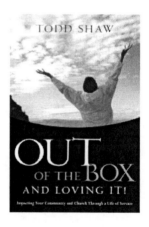

In *Out of the Box and Loving It*, Todd calls for a shift in the way Christians look at what ministry is and how it can be applied to those who most need it. With practical, pertinent ways to move the focus of ministry from "in the church" to "out of the church," this book provides guidance and encouragement to make a real impact on others in exciting and relevant ways.

This easy to follow guide allows the reader to discover and create a personal plan to reach others for Christ.

www.outoftheboxandlovingit.com

LaVergne, TN USA
13 February 2011
216400LV00005B/157/P